Bows and Arrows of the Greenland Thule Culture (1200–1900 AD)

A study of archaeological and ethnographic sources

Sebastian J. Pfeifer

BAR INTERNATIONAL SERIES 3060 | 2021

BAR
PUBLISHING

Published in 2021 by
BAR Publishing, Oxford

BAR International Series 3060

Bows and Arrows of the Greenland Thule Culture (1200–1900 AD)

ISBN 978 1 4073 5902 1 paperback
ISBN 978 1 4073 5903 8 e-format

DOI https://doi.org/10.30861/9781407359021

A catalogue record for this book is available from the British Library

BAR

PUBLISHING

BAR titles are available from:

BAR Publishing
122 Banbury Rd, Oxford, OX2 7BP, UK
 EMAIL info@barpublishing.com
 PHONE +44 (0)1865 310431
   FAX +44 (0)1865 316916
www.barpublishing.com

Of related interest

On the Hunt for Medieval Whales
Zooarchaeological, historical and social perspectives on cetacean exploitation in medieval northern and western Europe
Youri van den Hurk
Oxford, BAR Publishing, 2020

BAR International Series 2998

Norse in Newfoundland
A critical examination of archaeological research at the Norse site at L'Anse aux Meadows, Newfoundland
Janet E. Kay
Oxford, BAR Publishing, 2012

BAR International Series 2339

Pot/Potter Entanglements and Networks of Agency in Late Woodland Period (c. AD 900-1300) Southwestern Ontario, Canada
Christopher Michael Watts
Oxford, BAR Publishing, 2008

BAR International Series 1828

Hotel Grønland
Human use of caves and rock shelters in West Greenland
Clemens Pasda
Oxford, BAR Publishing, 2004

BAR International Series 1309

Settlement Archaeology in a Fjordland Archipelago
Network Analysis, Social Practice and the Built Environment of Western Vancouver Island, British Columbia, Canada since 2,000 BP
Quentin Mackie
Oxford, BAR Publishing, 2001

BAR International Series 926

Acknowledgments

This study would not have been possible without the dedicated support by Prof. Dr Bjarne Grønnow and Prof. Dr Hans Christian Gulløv who facilitated and supervised my work at the Arctic Center (SILA) at the Ethnographic Collections of the National Museum of Denmark, granted access to the objects in the permanent exhibition, patiently searched the depot for any archery-related finds and were always open for scientific and organisational questions. They also commented on earlier drafts of the manuscript. Mikkel Myrup (Greenland National Museum & Archives) kindly provided ample information on the bows and arrows that have been repatriated to Greenland. Many thanks also go to Dr Martin Appelt, Dr Peter Andreas Toft, Dr Jens Fog Jensen, Dr Ulla Odgaard, Dr Ditlev M. Mahler, and Tilo Krause for our fruitful discussions, their invaluable input as well as their literature tips. Nuka K. Godfredsen translated the terms in the works of Otto Fabricius into modern West Greenlandic. The welcoming and inspiring atmosphere at SILA contributed a lot to making my research stay to Copenhagen an outstanding scientific adventure! I thank very much Dr Jesper K. Nielsen (Natmus Copenhagen) for providing digitalised versions of photographs from the Fifth Thule Expedition, Wibeke Haldrup (Natmus Copenhagen) for providing digitalised versions of the Bergen and Copenhagen paintings of West Greenlanders and the permission to reproduce them, Hans Lange (Natmus Nuuk) for providing a digitalised version of a water colour by Aaron of Kangeq and the permission to reproduce it, Laura Søvsø Thomasen (Det Kgl. Bibliotek Copenhagen) for the permission to reproduce a map by Hans Egede, Shannon Mooney (Canadian Museum of History) for providing a digitalised version of a photograph of a Copper Inuit archer and the permission to reproduce it. I owe thanks to Lotte and Anders Glob for their kind permission to reproduce an image created by their father, Peter Valentin Glob as well as Louise and Thomas Birket-Smith for their kind permission to reproduce an image created by their grandfather, Kaj Birket-Smith. Janus Bahs Jaquet (Museum Tusculanum Press) and Prof. Dr Signe Arnfred (Roskilde) has to be thanked for their dedicated support in finding the heirs of the copyrights of pictures from old MoG issues. Despite our efforts, the present copyright holders of Fig. 3.2; 3.5–3.7 (by Søren Richter), and Fig. 3.8 (by Erik Holtved) could unfortunately not be identified. Thanks a lot to Dr Kenneth Ritchie (Moesgaard Museum) for proof reading. Two anonymous reviewers helped to improve the manuscript with their most appreciated comments. The BAR editorial and production team, in particular Jacqueline Senior, Lisa Eaton and Dr Ruth Fisher (Oxford), did a great job in guiding me through the publication process and always ensured that it ran absolutely smoothly. Our cooperation could not have been better. Last not least I want to acknowledge Prof. Dr Clemens Pasda (Friedrich Schiller University Jena) whose enthusiasm for the archaeology and ethnography of Greenland has opened up a whole new world for me as one of his students. I am indebted to the German Academic Exchange Service (DAAD) who generously supported my stay to Denmark in 2014 by a post-doc grant.

My sincere thanks to all of you!

Jena, October 2021
Sebastian J. Pfeifer

Contents

List of figures

List of maps

List of plates

List of tables

Abstract

The Thule Culture is the first Neo-Inuit culture in the North American Arctic. In Greenland as its easternmost distribution area, it existed from ca. 1200–1900 AD. The hunter-gatherers of the Greenland Thule culture, as their western neighbours, used the bow and arrow to a great extent for capturing large land mammals, preeminently caribou. This study aims to address the phenomenon of archery in the Eastern Arctic from an archaeological and ethnographic perspective. For this purpose, the archery-related artefacts attributed to the Thule tradition in the extensive archaeological and ethnographic collections of the National Museum of Denmark were systematically studied. Additionally, the rich ethno-historical record beginning with Danish colonisation activities in West Greenland in the early 18th century is taken into account. Based on a detailed catalogue recording provenance, raw materials, metric data and design, the archery of the Greenlandic Inuit is characterised technologically and culturally. Clearly, the Thule bows from Greenland are part of the very distinct holarctic Inuit archery tradition which becomes tangible with the evolution of the Thule culture in the Bering Strait region at around 1000 AD. Its features are 1) spliced or laminated composite bows from conifer compression wood, antler or baleen with complex profiles the most particular of which being the triple-curve, 2) a twisted or untwisted cable backing from raw hide or plaited sinew and 3) arrows with a tangential fletching, a wooden main shaft and a foreshaft or point from osseous material. In the case of Greenland, it becomes obvious that the regionally varying availability of suitable raw materials for bow and arrow manufacture triggered both design and dimensions: Whereas in Polar Greenland very short baleen and antler bows are typical, rather long wood bows were made in the more southern regions along the west and east coast. As far as chronology is concerned, the archery equipment has undergone some significant changes over the 700 years of Thule tradition. When the Thule pioneers reached Polar Greenland in the early 13th century they brought with them their typical short triple-curved composite bows. This complex design survived in Central West Greenland until the 17th century, where it co-existed with long and relatively simple d-bows that according to the material and ethno-historical record completely replaced it by the 18th century. This may or may not have to do with the increasing exposure to Europeans. Most certainly due to European contact are compound arrowheads with metal points that are attested from the 18th century onwards. In Northeast Greenland which was colonised from Polar Greenland during the 15th century, the triple-curved bow remained in use until the beginning of the 19th century. However, owing to the progressing climate-related geographical isolation of the regional Thule population, this design formally declined, and the methods of its manufacture changed. This work opens up new perspectives on how ballistic weapons of cold-adapted archaeological and historical hunter-gatherer societies can be analysed and interpreted – not only in the Arctic but all over the Northern hemisphere.

Introduction

The Thule culture is named after the settlement of Uummannaq (Thule) in Polar Greenland (Mathiassen 1927b). It is the first Neo-Inuit culture and directly precedes all recent Inuit societies of the North American Arctic (Raghavan et al. 2014). After its evolution in coastal North Alaska around 1000 AD it quickly spread eastwards (Friesen and Arnold 2008). Greenland as its easternmost distribution area was probably reached in the beginning of the 13th century (Gulløv 1997). In turn, the foundation of a missionary and trading station by Knud Rasmussen in 1909, again at Uummannaq, can be regarded as an upper temporal limit, marking a point in Greenland's history when Danish colonisation activities, which started in the early 1700s, had finally reached the most remote indigenous population. Hence the development of the Thule culture in Greenland covers around seven hundred years (Gulløv 2005).

The hunt was the backbone of Thule subsistence and therefore an extensive and complex assortment of specialised weapon systems for capturing a great variety of marine and terrestrial prey species existed (Fabricius 1818; Gulløv 1997; Hansen 1998). Bow and arrow were the single most important weapon set for hunting big land mammals, predominantly caribou and musk ox. Not surprisingly, already the pioneers of Greenland archaeology and ethnography, Kaj Birket-Smith, Erik Holtved, Helge Larsen, Therkel Mathiassen, Knud Rasmussen, Peter Valentin Glob, Hans Peder Steensby and Thomas Thomsen, paid considerable attention to that subject in their manifold works. In 1918, Birket-Smith published his seminal study *The Greenland Bow*. Being a compact overview which is based on examples in the collections of the National Museum of Denmark it presents the state of research at the beginning of the 20th century and provides a concise survey of the weapon's occurrence and variation in the different regions of Greenland.

The present study hence builds on a 100-year research tradition on Greenland archery. In doing so, it complements and further develops the work done by the pioneers but also adds important new information. First of all, detailed metric data as well as a thorough visual documentation of the original objects are presented. Second, the arrow as a complementary to the bow and equally important part of the weapon system will also be dealt with. Third, specifications about raw materials, design and technology are provided as this information is of great relevance for the classification and evaluation of archery equipment within the cultural context of its makers and users (Alix et al. 2012; Junkmanns 2013; Lepers and Rots 2020). Finally, continuous fieldwork and research carried out in Greenland

and other Arctic and Subarctic regions since Birket-Smith and his contemporaries have, of course, yielded many new finds and insights modifying their observations and conclusions significantly as well as putting them into a broader context. The revision of the chronology of the Thule migration into the Eastern Arctic (Friesen and Arnold 2008; Raghavan et al. 2014) and the ongoing discoveries of extensive archery equipment for caribou hunting from melting alpine ice patches in Northwest Canada since 1997 (Andrews et al. 2012; Hare et al. 2004) are two prominent examples. The backbone of this work is a catalogue with provenance, context, quantitative and qualitative data, as well as detailed illustrations of all accessible bows and arrows of the Greenland Thule culture held in the archaeological and ethnographic collections of the National Museum of Denmark in Copenhagen. In addition, the ethno-historical tradition, consisting of written sources and pictorial representations, is taken into account. On this basis, the typological diversity, regional variability, and chronological development of Greenlandic Thule archery will be discussed. A second focus of the study is on functional analysis. Design features such as profile, cross section, silhouette, and length result in characteristic shooting characteristics of the bow and flight behaviour of the arrow. These are not random, but reflect a technological tradition that – influenced by the main parameters of raw material, habitat characteristics, prey species and cultural conventions – aimed at producing highly optimised hunting weapons. Taking into account the current state of interdisciplinary research on projectile technology and recent materials scientific studies against a cultural scientific background (e.g. Margaris 2009 and 2014; Pfeifer et al. 2019), an attempt is made to decipher these complex interactions. Projectile technology plays a central role in archaeological and historic hunter-gatherer societies (e.g. Iovita and Sano 2016; Knecht 1997; Langley 2016), and thus the study of the archery of the Greenland Thule culture from a spatiotemporal and technological perspective can make an important contribution to our knowledge of the cultural history of the Eastern Arctic.

2

Background

2.1. Bow and arrow mechanics

A bow is a mechanical device that has two tasks: First, it must store energy by deformation when drawn. Second, it must transmit it to the arrow when the string is released. The theoretical foundations of bow mechanics were established around the middle of the 20th century (Beckhoff 1963; Elmer 1952; Hickman et al. 1947; Klopsteg 1947). In addition, a broad number of ballistic experiments addressing bow performance with – in rare cases – originals (Grayson 1993; Hamilton 1982; Hardy 1992; Pope 1923), or faithful replicas of varying historical designs have been conducted for a long time (e.g. Baker 1992; 1994; Barton and Bergman 1982; Bergman et al. 1988; Callahan 2001; Hamm 1991; Insulander 1999; Junkmanns 2013; Lepers and Rots 2020; Miller et al. 1986; Paulsen 1999; Stodiek 1993). Computer assisted modelling (Kooi 1991; Kooi and Bergman 1997; Riesch 2002) is the most recent method for assessing bow design and performance. This enduring and multi-faceted research tradition has after all produced a good understanding of how a bow works (Baker 1992; 1994; Lepers and Rots 2020).

2.1.1. Energy storage

The energy storage capacity of a bow can be visualised in a *force-draw diagram* (Klopsteg 1947) (Fig. 2.1): On the x axis, the draw length is plotted, on the y axis the force. During the drawing process, the f-d curve will run from bottom left to top right. The surface under the curve represents the stored potential energy (Beckhoff 1963, fig. 3.3). Basically, the curve can be straight – meaning a linear increase of the force during the draw (Fig. 2.1a), concave – meaning an exponential increase (Fig. 2.1b), and convex – meaning an exponential approach (Fig. 2.1c). Consequently, most energy is stored by a bow with a convex f-d curve, least by a bow with a concave one (Baker 1992, 70).

The energy storing capacity of a bow is influenced by a number of factors the four most important of which will be discussed in the following.

Draw weight

The more force it takes to bend a bow's limbs to a given draw length, the more energy is stored (Baker 1992, 45). Traditionally, the draw weight is measured in English pounds (lbs). One pound equals 0.454 kg. For example, a draw weight of 50 lbs equals a weight of 22.7 kg hanging on the string to fully bend the bow.

Draw length

The greater the draw length of a bow, the more energy is stored because its limbs travel farther. Baker (1992, 46) chronographed several wood bows of equal design and draw weight (45 lbs), but with different draw lengths: A 56 cm draw bow shot the arrow with a speed of 39 meter per second, whereas a 66 cm draw bow cast the same arrow 42 m per second.

Bow length

The longer a bow, the more energy is stored: In another experiment carried out by Baker (1992, 69), a 122 cm long d-bow drawing 50 pounds at 71 cm draw length cast the arrow with a speed of 41 meters per second. A 168 cm long bow of the same weight, draw length and design outshot it by almost 6 meters per second. Why is that? In a short d-bow, the angle between the tips and the string is much bigger at full draw than in a longer bow with the result of a less favourable lever. Thus, it becomes much harder to bend when approaching full draw. This so-called stacking (Junkmanns 2013, 55; fig. 34) results in a concave f-d curve (Fig. 2.1b), whereas the longer bow produces a more or less straight one (Fig. 2.1a).

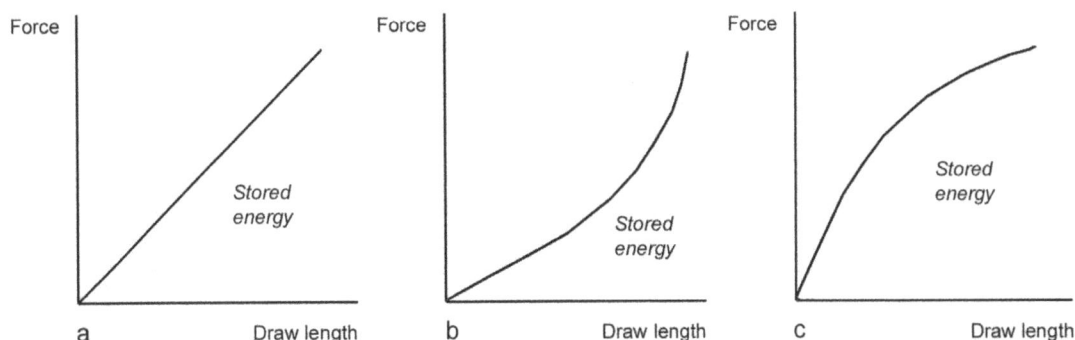

Fig. 2.1 Different force-draw curves of bows.

Profile

A high energy-storing bow has a convex f-d curve, reflecting a high early draw weight but a low increase of it in the end of the draw (Baker 1992, 49) (Fig. 2.1c). A high early draw weight, i.e. a bow which is hard to bend in the beginning, can be accomplished by pre-stressing the bow stave before the actual drawing process begins: Even the limbs of a simple straight d-bow are under a certain degree of initial strain when the string is put on, as they had to move a few centimetres from their relaxed position. If the bow is additionally reflexed and/or recurved, initial strain will be even higher as the limbs have to travel comparatively farther to be strung (Kooi and Bergman 1997, fig. 2.4). Recurved ends have yet another important benefit in a bow: They keep the string angle low. The recurved bow is actually a short bow becoming longer during the draw when the string lifts off the recurves (Beckhoff 1963, 77). Depending on length, angle and design of the recurves, this is the most energy-storing bow profile. Traditional Ottoman and Korean bows, for example, many of which being designed explicitly for long distance shooting competitions and able to cast an arrow over half a mile (Karpowicz 2007; Klopsteg 1947), literally uncoil when strung and drawn (Bergman and McEwen 1997, fig. 3).

2.2.2. Energy transmission

When the bow is shot, a substantial part of the potential energy stored in the limbs is turned into kinetic energy that, again, is transmitted to the arrow (Kooi and Bergman 1997, 125). The degree of effectiveness of this process is reflected in arrow speed and consequently shooting distance (Bergman et al. 1988). The main conditioning factor is the mass of the moving parts (Kooi and Bergman 1997, 132).

Limb mass

Light limbs move more quickly than heavy ones. In wooden bows, a mass difference of 30 g can affect the arrow speed by about 0.3 meters per second (Baker 1992, 65). Knowing this, it becomes obvious why there is an upper limit for effective bow length: In an example presented by Baker (1992, 69 f.), a 240 cm long d-bow owing to its very low string angle stores much more potential energy at 70 cm draw length than a 170 cm bow with the same profile. However, due to its much higher mass it casts the arrow only 41 meters per second while the shorter and therefore lighter bow casts it 47 meters per second. Generally speaking, a composite bow assembled from wood, glue and animal tissue has a considerably higher relative mass than a wooden self bow. To compensate, it has to be short and it must have a high energy-storing profile (Kooi and Bergman 1997, 133). In shooting experiments carried out by Bergman et al. (1988, 666; tab. 1), a highly reflexed and recurved Crimean Tartar composite of wood, sinew and horn cast a 50 g arrow as much as 90 m farther than a much stronger yew self longbow with a d-profile using the same draw length of 81 cm. In contrast, a replica of a Pharaonic Egyptian composite bow of wood, horn and sinew with a simple d-profile – despite of having much greater un-braced reflex and draw length – did not have better cast than the yew self bow because its very high mass offset all benefits from superior energy storage.

Mass placement

The parts of the bow that travel farthest should have the lowest mass (Kooi and Bergman 1997, 132). Consequently, a limb silhouette which is widest at the handle section and narrowest at the tips is more mass-efficient than one with parallel sides or even widened tips (Baker 1992, 66 f.).

String mass

Like the limbs, the bow string should be as light as possible. Tests carried out by Baker (1992, 73) suggest that 1/3 of string mass increase slows down the arrow speed by about 1.5 meters per second.

Arrow mass

The lighter the arrow is, the faster and farther it will fly (Bergman / McEwen / Miller 1988, tab. 1; Elmer 1952, 264; Junkmanns 2013, fig. 39; Miller / McEwen / Bergman 1986, 188).

As explained above, the optimal bow design combines low mass, a long draw length and a high energy-storing profile (Klopsteg 1947, 156). Modern bows made from high-performance materials like fibreglass or carbon fibre are far more efficient than bows made of traditional materials (Lepers and Rots 2020). However, mechanical efficiency is not the single most important consideration in a weapon system that has to be adapted to a certain environment and particular hunting techniques: A 150 cm d-bow, for instance, might be less effective than one being 180 cm long, but it requires less raw material and is more maneuverable. A shorter draw length might store less energy, but the shooting process is faster and the arrow can also be shorter. A d-bow might be less effective than a recurve, but is more stable, accurate and far easier to make. Overbuilt bow tips may slow down cast, but are less likely to fail than more delicate ones. Though a light arrow has the potential to fly faster than a heavy projectile, to really benefit from its low mass it needs a corresponding bow with light, quick reacting limbs. A slow bow with a high draw weight very often does not cast a light arrow farther than a fast bow with a much lower draw weight (Bergman et al. 1988). On the other hand, a heavy and therefore more inert arrow gives a bow with more slowly moving limbs enough time to transmit its kinetic energy (Baker 1992, 66; Lepers and Rots 2020, 4). And even though this heavy arrow will fly comparatively slowly, it will nevertheless have a lot of momentum owing to its high mass. In traditional archery, heavier projectiles tend to have more effect on the target than lighter, faster ones (Junkmanns 2013, 57). A spear thrown with an atlatl is much slower than an arrow and will never fly as far (Bergman et al. 1988, fig.

2.5; Cattelain 1997, 226; Stodiek 1993, 196). However, owing to its much higher mass it provides a greater impact force than any arrow could (Bergman et al. 1988, 666). Apart from impact a more massive projectile is also less fragile and, moreover, reported to be less affected by wind (Bohr 1998, 79). These considerations suggest that the objective assessment of archaeological and ethnographic bows and arrows requires a holistic approach (Kooi and Bergman 1997, 134), equally factoring in mechanical and technological as well as cultural and environmental variables (Baker 1994).

2.2. Terminology and classification of Arctic bows and arrows

The terminology of Arctic bow and arrow parts applied in this study is adapted from Bergman et al. (1988), Hare et al. (2004), and Murdoch (1890) (Fig. 2.2):

Regarding the profile of the strung bow, four different basic versions are encountered in the Arctic (Fig. 2.3). The terms *d-bow*, *recurved bow* and *double-curved bow* are established and widely accepted terms in archery research (Baker 1994; Cattelain 1997; Hamilton 1982; Junkmanns 2013). In addition to these, there is a particular Arctic bow profile, for which no naming currently exists. Therefore, the term *triple-curved* is being introduced here. The *d-bow* has a continuous curve throughout its length in the shape of a circle segment. This is the simplest profile. In a *recurved bow*, the ends are bent forward at an angle and point in shooting direction. There are rigid recurves, traditionally referred to as *siyahs* (Grayson 1993, 119 ff.), and working recurves which uncoil during the draw (Baker 1992, 61). The *double-curved bow* has a reflexed handle section and deflexed limbs. In the *triple-curved* bow, the bend is distributed over a big curve in the middle and two smaller ones at the ends. There are countless variations of

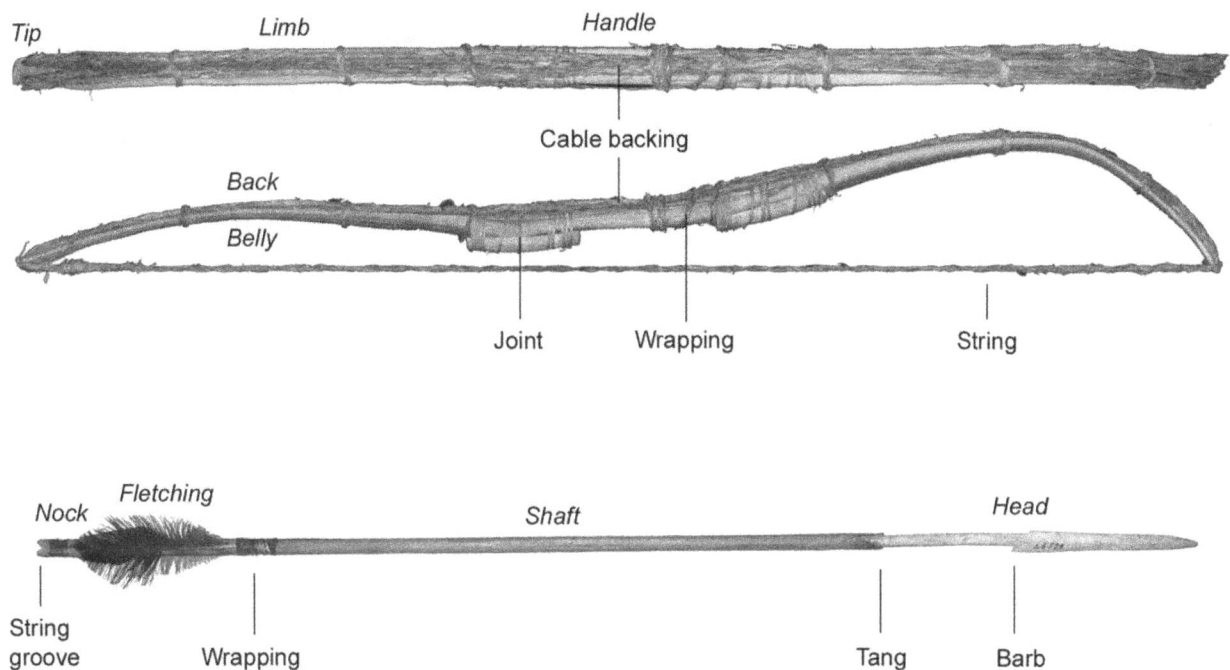

Fig. 2.2 Arctic bow and arrow parts. No scale.

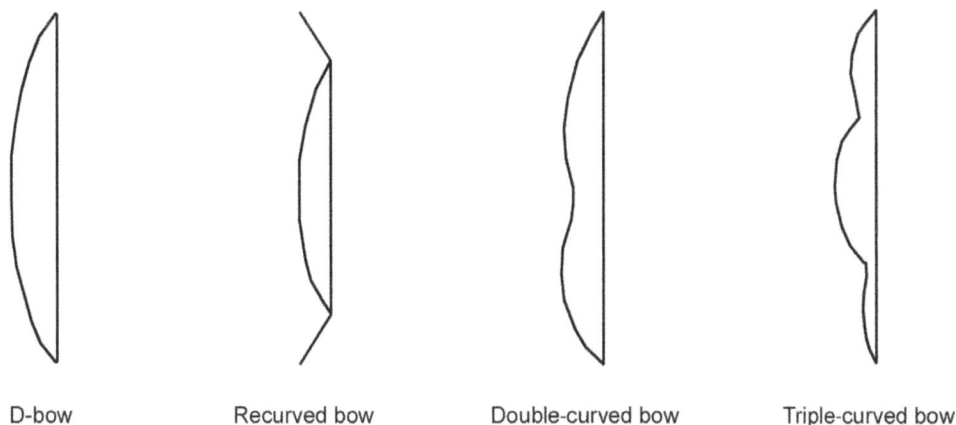

Fig. 2.3 Arctic bow profiles.

these four profiles as to length and angle of the recurves and triple curves, severity of reflex, rigidity of the handle section, and limb symmetry (Murdoch 1890).

While the first three bow profiles are generally spread all over the world (Baker 1994; Cattelain 1997; Roth 2004), the triple-curved bow is a purely Arctic phenomenon. Some scholars interpret it as a vestigial descendent of the Asian recurve bow (Bergman and McEwen 1997, 158; Grayson 1993, 152; Hamilton 1982, 84).

In terms of manufacturing and technology, Arctic bows can be categorically divided into self bows, whose staves are made of a single piece of material, and composite bows, whose staves are composed of several parts (Fig. 2.4). Among composite bows, in turn, there is the laminated composite, the stave of which being composed of long horizontal layers, and the spliced composite, which consists of modules arranged in line. This classification departs to some extent from more traditional definitions that use the term self bow exclusively for plain wood bows and suggest that a composite bow stave should always contain animal raw material, primarily horn and sinew (*sensu* McEwen et al. 1991). As Arctic bows categorically have a backing of animal tissue (see 2.3.3.), they would all be classified as composite bows in this reading, but this generic term does not do justice to their diversity. To date, there is no universal consensus on technology-based bow classification (see Baker 1994; Beckhoff 1963; Bergman et al. 1988; Bergmann and McEwen 1997, 148; Cattelain 1997; Grayson 1993; Kooi and Bergman 1997; Lepers and Rots 2020), and as the terms are very loose to begin

with, it is justified to modify the traditional terminology to describe the technological variability of Arctic bow staves as accurately and unambiguously as possible without being too detailed and thus confusing.

The Arctic arrow shaft (Fig. 2.2) is always made of wood and characterised by a flattened proximal end with a broadened nock. The arrowhead may either be made in one piece or assembled of an osseous (mammal bone, caribou antler, walrus and narwhale tusk – comp. Langley 2016; Pfeifer et al. 2019) foreshaft and an inset tip of stone or metal. Concerning the fletching, there are the *radial* and the *tangential* fletching method. The radial fletching usually consists of three, sometimes two or four, split feathers attached in a variety of ways (Lepers and Rots 2020) whereas the tangential fletching is made from two whole feathers applied oppositely on either side of the shaft (Birket-Smith 1948, 118). The radial fletching method, extremely prevalent in prehistoric and historical times in Europe (Hardy 2006; Junkmanns 2013); the Near East (Miller et al. 1986), Africa (Cattelain 1997; Roth 2004), and North America (Bohr 1998 and 2000; Hamm 1991; Hamilton 1982; Hare et al. 2004) is remarkably rare in the Arctic though (Jenness 1946, 126).

Throughout the North American Arctic, bows and arrows were stored and carried in a combined quiver-bow case made of waterproof leather, which in most cases also contained a pouch for tools and rations. It features a short wooden or osseous handle as well as a long back strap (Birket-Smith 1945, fig. 18; 1948, fig. 38; Jenness 1946, fig. 3.87).

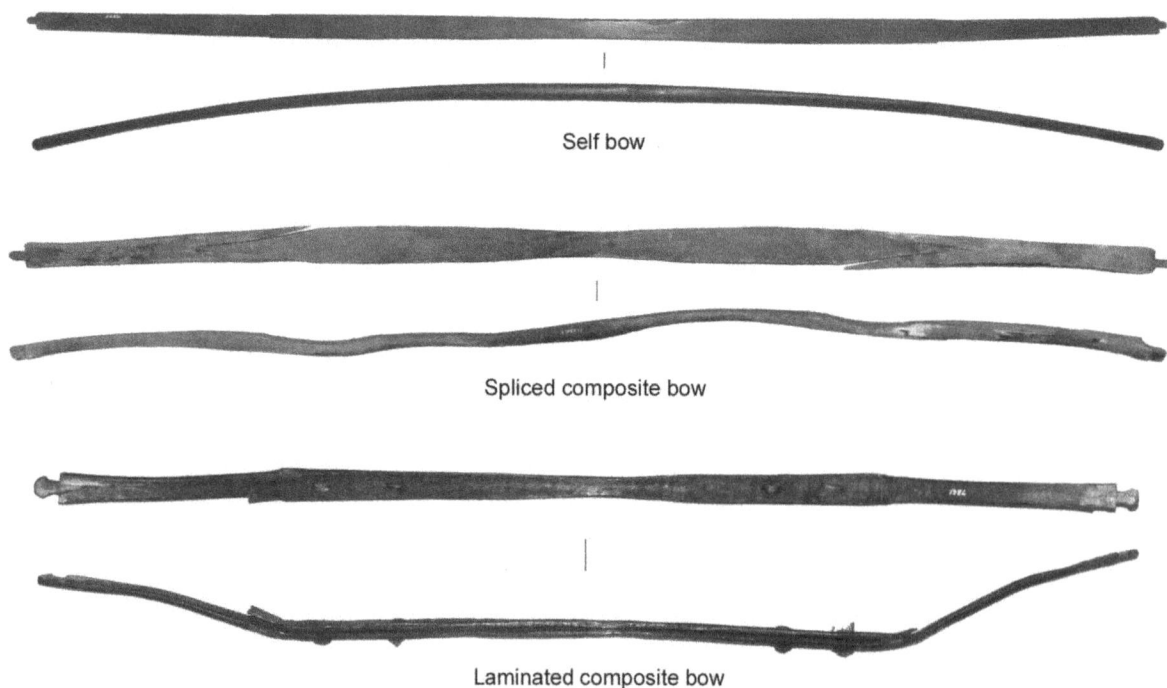

Self bow

Spliced composite bow

Laminated composite bow

Fig. 2.4 Arctic bow staves classified according to technology. No scale.

2.3. Characteristics of Arctic archery technology

Generally, the bowyers of the North American Arctic faced three main challenges resulting from the environment they were living in: 1. the scarcity of suitable raw materials for the bow stave, 2. the lack of convenient glues for joints, and 3. frequently very low temperatures. To deal with them, a distinctive archery technology evolved (Birket-Smith 1948, 117 ff.; Grayson 1993, 149 f.; Murdoch 1890; Thomsen 1928, 320 ff.)

2.3.1. Raw materials

Driftwood

Conifer driftwood was the prevailing raw material for both bows and arrows (Alix 2009; Fienup-Riordan 2007, 61; Murdoch 1890, 307). Different kinds of wood were expertly chosen for their individual properties (Petersen 1986, 18). Though sheer quantities and sizes of driftwood on Arctic shores can be considerable, much too often a promising looking log is actually cracked, decayed, or partially eaten by invertebrates (Grønnow 1996, 78). Moreover, during the drying process wood can warp and crack and hence become useless as well. Therefore, high-quality driftwood pieces clean of irregularities and with a straight grain are typically short and narrow (Alix 2009).

Antler

The compacta of antler is a hard, heavy and extraordinarily tough osseous raw material. Tests carried out on Greenland caribou antler (*Rangifer tarandus groenlandicus*) revealed a mean longitudinal bending strength of 336 MPa (Pfeifer et al. 2019). This is about the same as measured for e.g. bovine femur (Chen et al. 2008, 217), but antler has a much higher work of fracture which means that it is able to absorb more energy by deformation before failing. From a mechanical point of view, antler is therefore ideal for both bow staves (Grayson 1993, 141) and arrowheads (Margaris 2014). Yet, it never grows in straight pieces which are long enough for a self bow stave and it is not easily worked with simple hand tools either. Soaking in water or urine for a longer time softens the material and allows for modifying its shape (Möller 1981–83).

Whalebone

Like caribou antler, whalebone played an important role for fittings of paddles and harpoons as well as for harpoon, dart and lance foreshafts (Gulløv 1997). Regarding dimensions, it provides much bigger pieces with which to work. Occasionally, whalebone was also used for the staves of spliced composites (Pl. 9). Little is known about the mechanical properties of that material, but it appears to be about as tough and flexible as antler (Malgaris 2009; 2014; Pétillon 2013, 541).

Horn and baleen

Musk ox horn was frequently used for bow staves in High Arctic regions where wood is extremely scarce (Birket-Smith 1945, 50). Due to the small dimensions of the raw material, horn bows always have to be spliced together from at least two pieces (Grayson 1993, 151).

Baleen mainly came from the bowhead whale (*Balaena mysticetus*) and was procured either by whale hunting or from carcasses (Thomsen 1928, 320). Baleen planks are slightly curved, and can be up to 4 m long and 0.2 m wide (Comstock 1992, 254). Both horn and baleen are composed of tightly packed, longitudinally running calcified keratin fibres (Szewciw et al. 2010). The material is heavy, softer than antler and very pliable. The amount of energy that can be stored per unit of mass by elastic deformation is considerably higher than in the best bow woods (Kooi and Bergman 1997, tab. 2). By cooking, steaming or application of dry heat, keratin polymers can be bent quite easily to any desired shape without losing their strength. This is important for making recurves and also because horn almost always grows spirally twisted (Grayson 1993, 144).

Hide

The tough skin of various seal species, especially the bearded seal (*Erignathus barbatus*) was frequently used for the cable backing (Birket-Smith 1918, 11). Rawhide is widely known as an excellent material for wood bow backings (Comstock 1992, 240).

Sinew

Sinew could be obtained from the caribou and from different whales and seals. Though there certainly are quality differences between the species (Birket-Smith 1918, 11), sinew has the highest energy storage potential of all biological raw materials (Kooi and Bergman 1997, tab. 2).

Feathers

Various Arctic bird species provide feathers that are big enough for the tangential fletching (Muus et al. 1990, 159 ff.).

Metal

European iron or steel was intensely used for arrow points as soon as it became available, either from Norse or colonial contacts (Gulløv 1997, 250 ff.; 2016). Additionally, meteorite iron from Cape York in the Thule region was also frequently worked (Buchwald 2001, 86 ff.). Copper, iron and brass were used for rivets.

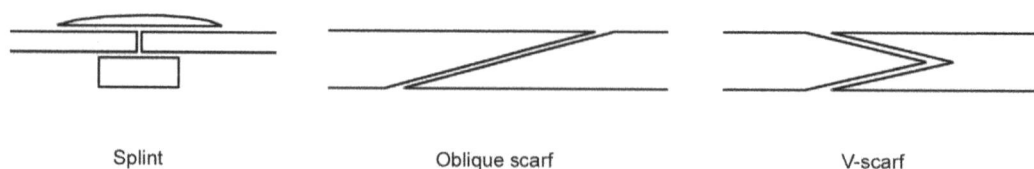

Splint   Oblique scarf   V-scarf

Fig. 2.5 Joints in Arctic spliced composite bows and arrows.

Stone

Stone was made into arrow points before metal was available or where it was scarce. Most often slate was used because it could easily be split into thin layers and then honed to a sharp edge (Tuborg Sandell and Sandell 1991).

2.3.2. Joining techniques

As has become clear, in many cases the raw material was not available in pieces big enough to make a self bow stave and therefore had to be joined (Fig. 2.5). Apart from that, in recurved bows (Fig. 2.3 and 2.4), it can actually be more convenient and durable to splice the recurves onto the stave instead of heat bending them into it. Concerning the arrow, the challenge was to connect arrowhead, i.e. point or foreshaft, and main shaft firmly, or even to assemble the latter from several pieces.

Splint

This joint appears exclusively on bow staves. Both flat-ended stave sections are reinforced by a long, flat bracer on the upper and a short, thick one on the lower side (Baker 1994, 86 f.; Grayson 1993, 151; Taylor 1972, 57) (Pl. 3: Lu. 324).

Scarfs

Basically, there is the oblique scarf and the v-scarf (Taylor 1972, 59). Though more time consuming to make, the latter is stronger as it provides a bigger contact surface, and it is also less prone to shifting. Compared to the splint, the scarf tends to be less elastic. Oblique scarfs are applied predominantly on arrows (e.g. Pl. 3: Lu. 327b) while v-scarfs are very common in bows (e.g. Pl. 3: L 1.4293).

The joints were fixed either by wrapping (Pl. 3: Lu. 324), or by sewing which required drilling holes (Pl. 3: L 17.88; Lc. 356). For the arrows, the distal ends typically form closed sockets to accommodate the matching screw or knob tangs of the corresponding points and foreshafts (Pl. 3: Lb. 579; Lu. 704). In rare cases, the tang of the point was set into the split distal end and then wrapped (Pl. 3: Lu. 323d). Metal points were attached to the foreshafts by rivets (Pl. 3: Lu. 327b).

2.3.3. The cable backing

Every single Arctic adult bow has a so-called backing, meaning a layer of sinew or rawhide attached to its back. Birket-Smith's (1918, 21) notion of un-backed Greenlandic laminated baleen bows is based on grave finds which are not in their original condition anymore (Grayson 1993, 152; 154). Similar baleen bows from the Western Arctic are invariably backed (Mathiassen 1927b, 43). Doubtless, the main task of the backing is to handle the tension forces on the back of the bow when it is bent, as the materials of the Arctic bow staves are either weak in tension – like conifer wood – or quite easily permanently deformed – like antler and baleen. Therefore, they need to be supported. Backing a bow stave with highly tensile material has yet other benefits (Baker 1992, 105 ff.). First, it renders a comparatively shorter weapon possible: A sinew-backed wood bow allows a draw length of as much as 50 percent of its length and a backed baleen or antler bow can be even shorter (Baker 1994, 86). A short bow is more maneuverable and, given a high energy-storing (e.g. recurved) profile, is also more efficient owing to its lower mass (see 2.2.2.). Second, the backing pulls the unstrung bow into a reflex, resulting in a higher early draw weight when strung and drawn. Third, the backing greatly strengthens the joints in a spliced or laminated composite bow. A rawhide or sinew backing is normally glued to the bow (Bergman and McEwen 1997). But in the Arctic strong animal hide glues required for that task were apparently not produced, possibly because the available hide types were not suited to glue cooking, or because of the risk of glue getting brittle at very low temperatures. Therefore, the backing is always a cable backing composed of several strands of either raw hide or plaited sinew fibres fastened to the bow by means of tying and wrapping. This tradition goes back to at least the first Neo-Inuit Punuk culture in the Bering Sea region (Gulløv 2005, 206). The cable backing is possibly the most distinctive feature of Arctic bows and the ingenuity of it has impressed ethnographers ever since (Egede 1741, 354; Fabricius 1818, 235; Birket-Smith 1948, 114; Porsild 1915a, 158). It is not an easy task to decipher the complex network of strands running up and down and around an Arctic bow. J. Murdoch (1890) was the first who explicitly analysed the cable backings of bows from the Western Arctic from a technological perspective and who classified them after their construction methods. Birket-Smith (1918) applied and modified this classification system to the Eastern Arctic. 100 years later, these observations are in principle still valid. There are two different cable backings: the Eastern type and the Arctic type. The terms 'Eastern' and 'Arctic' do by no means refer to their geographical distribution as they often exist side by side (Fig. 2.6).

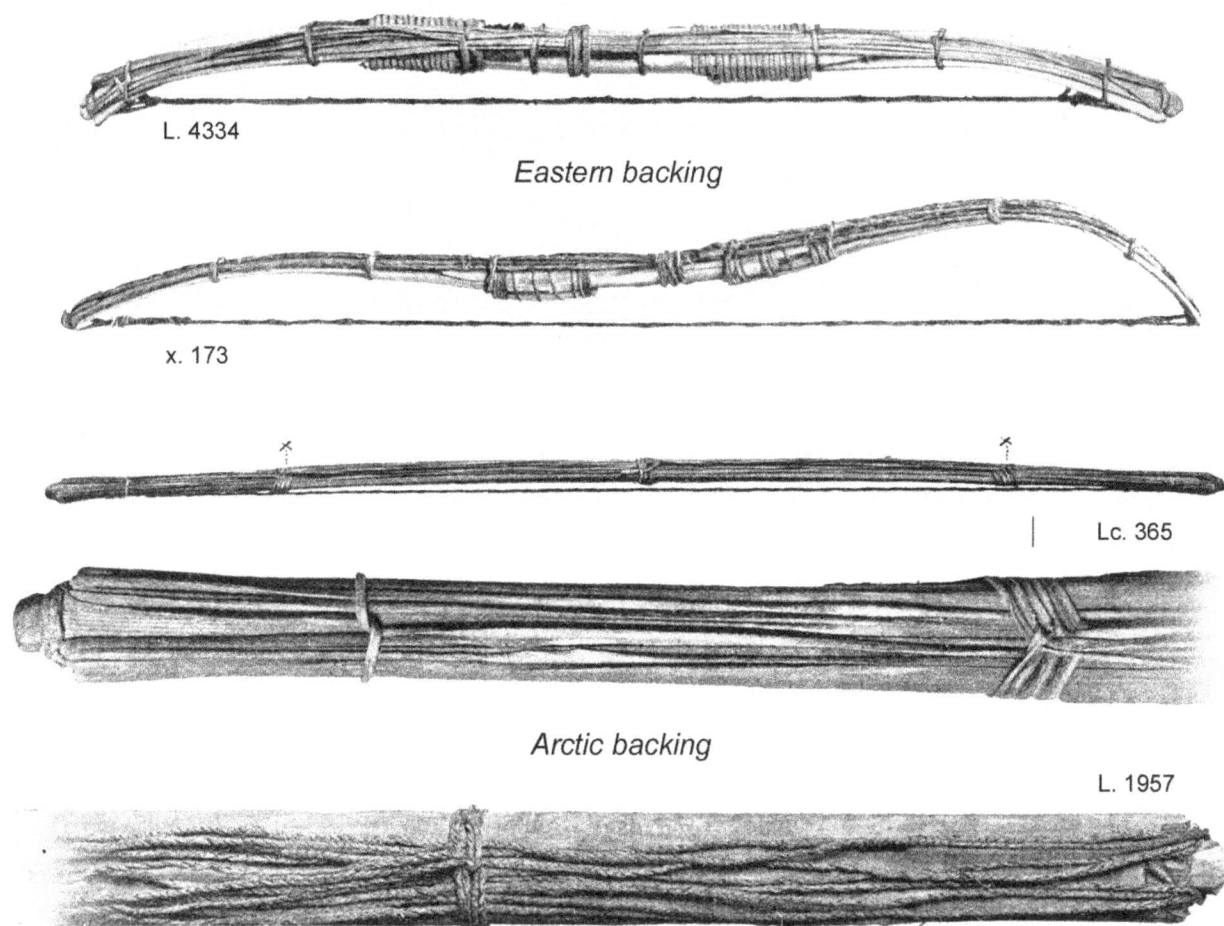

L. 4334

Eastern backing

x. 173

Lc. 365

Arctic backing

L. 1957

Fig. 2.6 Backing types in the Eastern Arctic (after Birket-Smith 1918, fig. 1b and c; 2b and c). Reproduced courtesy of Louise and Thomas Birket-Smith.

The Eastern type (Birket-Smith 1918, 13; Murdoch 1890, 308) is characterised by one single cable running from tip to tip and fixed to the bow stave by lashings. The number of cable strands remains the same along the whole length of the bow. The Arctic type is more complex as it consists of two layers (Murdoch 1890, 310 ff.; pl. IV). Birket-Smith's (1918, 19 f.; fig. 2b) description of the Arctic cable backing using the example of a specimen from West Greenland (Fig. 2.6) is unsurpassed in its clearness and instructiveness and will therefore be quoted here in full length:

"The backing consists of a long sealhide line in three strips knotted together. It is fastened to the one nock by a running noose, and passed thence three times back and forth between the points; the fourth time it is only carried one way the whole length, and then back for 10 cm. from the point, where it is fastened round stave and backing with a half-knot, which may be taken as the termination of the lower layer. The thong is now carried along to the nearest shoulder, where it again forms a half-knot, making the commencement of the upper layer, and thence on again to the second shoulder, where it is carried round the stave in a sling; now running back to the first shoulder again it makes another sling, etc. so that at last we have at the one shoulder, 1 half-knot and

3 slings, at the second, 4 slings. Finally, the loose end is carried in a half-knot and made fast round the grip."

Consequently, this backing technique results in about twice as many strands in the middle part of the bow than at the ends, which means that it is extra reinforced. Very often, the individual cable strands were combined into one or two thick bundles and then twisted (Jenness 1946, 122). That was done by using a pair of so-called cable twisters of wood, ivory or antler. Throughout the Arctic, those tools were a common part of archery equipment (Thomsen 1928, 321) (Fig. 2.7). There is ample ethno-historic information on their daily use, together with a pair of marlin spikes, to constantly adjust the cable backing to specific moisture conditions and to relax it when the bow was not in use (Jenness 1922, fig. 2.43; Stefánsson 1914, 96; fig. 39).

Yet, twisting does not always occur. Many Eastern and some Arctic cable backings were definitely not twisted (Birket-Smith 1918, fig. 1; 1929, 103; 1945, 56) (Fig. 2.6: Lc. 365), and if the cable was permanently tied down to the stave to prevent slipping by means of several half hitches in regular intervals (e.g. Murdoch 1890, pl. II; V; IX,22), there was anyway no possibility either to re-adjust or to relax it without totally disintegrating the whole backing.

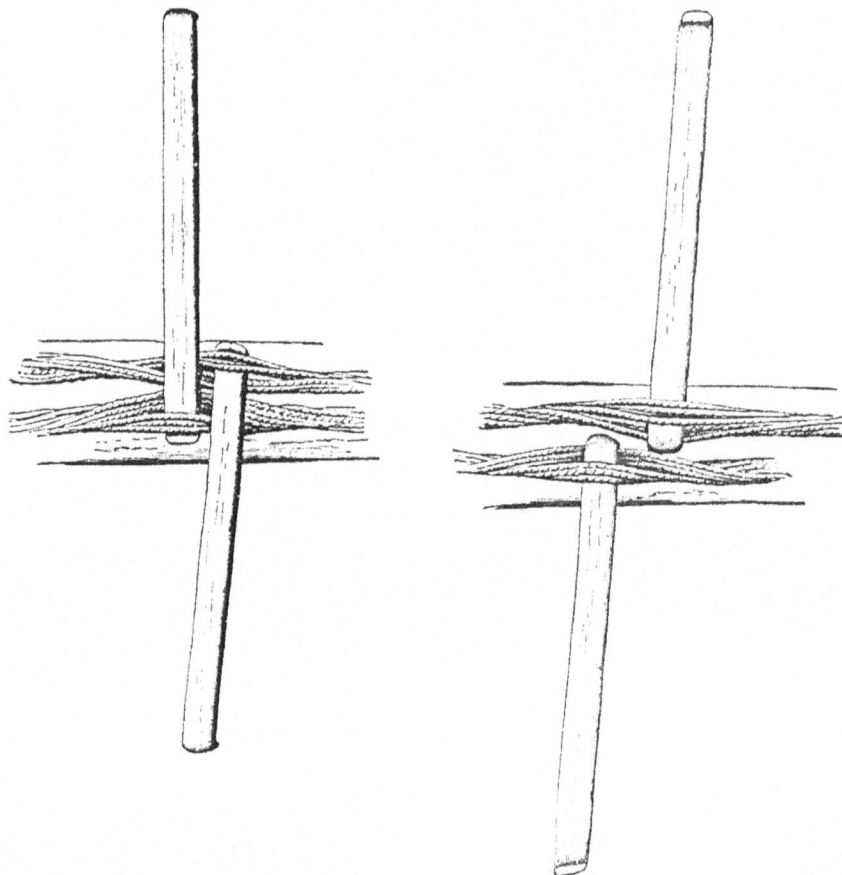

Fig. 2.7 Application of cable twisters (Murdoch 1890, pl. XI).

2.3.4. Tools and manufacturing process

The manifold and diverse working of wood and osseous raw materials amongst traditional Arctic cultures required a surprisingly small tool kit and simple workplace (Fienup-Riordan 2007, 66 ff.). Driftwood logs were split by means of heavy wedges, very often of tough antler and whalebone (Gulløv 1997, 171). Adzes of different sizes and weights with stone and later metal blades were used for roughing out the principal shape of the bow stave (Birket-Smith 1918, 11; Petersen 1986, 17). For the finer work on the bow and for making arrow shafts either a simple knife was used or the long-handled knife. This special tool with a short, single-bevelled and often curved blade was drawn towards the body following the grain, producing thin shavings very much like a smoothing plane (Petersen 1986, 17). The so-called tillering is the most difficult task during the bow making process. By removing small portions of material on the belly, an even bend of the limbs is accomplished, resulting in the desired profile and draw weight (Hamm 1992). The final polishing of the bow stave and of the osseous arrowheads to an almost mirror-like finish removed work traces and irregularities. This was probably accomplished with fine-grained stones or the coarse skin of some fish species. Regular holes, needed for joints and sometimes also for the preparation of pre-forms (Birket-Smith 1918, 11; Gulløv 1997, 246), were

made using the bow drill. The arrow fletching was cut to shape with the aid of small wooden feather cutting boards (Mathiassen 1945, 58; fig. 29). In many cases, heat bending was required either to straighten the work piece or to give it a desired shape. Dry heat in combination with greasy substances works well on thin wooden objects like arrow shafts (Bohr 1998, 76). However, when thick pieces like recurves in bow staves had to be formed, steam bending was the prevalent method (Fienup-Riordan 2007, 66). It is also gentler to the material and more durable than dry heat (Comstock 1993a). Perforated bone or antler batons of various sizes served as levers (Birket-Smith 1929, fig. 23; Jenness 1946, fig. 172–174; Stefánsson 1914, fig. 2.40).

Thule culture archery in Greenland

3.1. The corpus: spatial distribution, find context, and preservation

Seventy-two individual bows attributed to the Greenland Thule Culture were included in this study (Appendix A1). Forty-one bows, including two specimens pictured on oil paintings from the 17th and 18th centuries, are housed in the archaeological and ethnographic collections of the National Museum of Denmark and were examined first-hand and documented in detail. Thirty-one bows could not be studied in the original and were therefore assessed from the literature. This group includes, on the one hand, specimens that were not accessible at the time of the study or that had been repatriated to the Greenland National Museum and Archives in Nuuk. Most noteworthy are the majority of finds recovered during the Danish East Greenland Expedition (1891–1892), the Carlsberg Expedition (1898–1900) and the Danmark Expedition (1906–1908), the excavations by Søren Richter in Northeast Greenland (1929–1930), as well as the biggest part of the Porsild collection from Disko. On the other hand, there are the bow finds originating from the Cambridge East Greenland Expedition (1926), the Bartlett East Greenland Expedition (1930), and the expedition led by Alfred Gabriel Nathorst (1899) which are now in the UK, the USA, and Sweden, respectively.

Seventy archaeological and ethnographic arrows from the Greenland Thule culture are included, 55 of which could be studied in detail (Appendix A2). Additionally the two paintings mentioned above were studied, a collection of single antler arrowheads from West Greenland (Appendix A11), and a set of 18 arrows from Ellesmere Island. Unaccessible or repatriated specimens are represented by 15 pieces, including the important early arrow Lc. 32b from the former Royal Kunstkammer whose removal from the exhibition showcase was not advisable for curatorial reasons. The extensive archaeological material from the early Thule culture sites of Uummannaq, Aunartoq, Nuulliit, Ruin Island, Kap Kent, Inuarfissuaq and Inussuk in Polar and Northwest Greenland, from Dødemandsbugten site in Northeast Greenland, as well as a substantial part of the finds from Illutalik, Sermermiut, Qeqertarmiut, Kangeq and Illorpaat in Central West Greenland are now housed in the Greenland National Museum and were therefore also not studied first-hand. Hence, all information was extracted from the literature and precise numbers or measurements cannot be provided here. Based on the information in the records of the National Museum of Denmark and the literature, most objects can be attributed relatively precisely to a region or even a certain place (Appendix A1 and 2; Map 1 and 2). However, for some of them, especially arrows, only

a rough allocation is possible. As can be clearly seen, their spatial distribution is very heterogeneous. First, the evidence of archery equipment in Greenland matches the main distribution of the caribou in Thule, Inglefield Land, Disko Bay and Nuuk Fjord, and of caribou and musk ox in Northeast Greenland (Meldgaard 1986, 8 ff.; fig. 2.6), respectively. In South and Southeast Greenland, on the other hand, where caribou have always been scarce or absent, there are hardly any finds (Birket-Smith 1918, 6). As bows and arrows were primarily used to hunt these two prey species, such a strong correlation has to be expected. Against that background, it is conspicuous that the Sisimiut district, for centuries one of the most important caribou hunting areas in West Greenland (Grønnow et al. 1983), despite intensive fieldwork yielded not a single bow. A possible explanation for this lack of finds could be the poor preservation conditions for organic objects in the relatively fertile Low Arctic areas with rich ground vegetation (comp. Pfeifer 2014, 18). For *Polar Greenland*, encompassing the Thule region, Inglefield Land and Peary Land, extensive archaeological and ethnographic evidence of archery equipment mainly originates from the long-term fieldwork carried out by Holtved (1944; 1954), Knuth (1952; 1981), and Steensby (1910). For *Northwest Greenland*, extending northward from Qeqertarsuup Tunua (Disko Bay) including Qeqertarsuaq (Disko Island) and Nuussuaq Peninsula, Mathiassen's excavations at Inussuk (1930) and Porsild's (1915a) collections from Disko are most noteworthy. From *Central West Greenland*, the area between Disko Bay and Nuuk Fjord, there is, on the one hand, the material from the archaeological sites of Illutalik (Mathiassen 1934), Sermermiut (Mathiassen 1958), and Qeqertarmiut (Mathiassen 1931) and from the more recent excavations at Kangeq and Illorpaat (Gulløv 1997). On the other hand, there are quite numerous finds acquired by Danish officials in the southern Disko Bay during the 19th century. In addition, from Nuuk Fjord there are some ethnographic bows and arrows collected by early European whalers and missionaries. In *Northeast Greenland*, stretching from Nordostrundingen down to Kangertittivaq (Scoresby Sund) many more or less scientific expeditions by different nationalities (Bartlett 1931; Mathiassen 1929; Nathorst 1900; Richter 1934; Ryder 1895; Thomsen 1917) were carried out at the end of the 19th and beginning of the 20th century (Grønnow 2010; Grønnow and Jensen 2003; Higgins 2010; Sørensen and Gulløv 2012). Archery equipment was typically collected from the surface in abandoned settlements or removed from graves. Additionally, there is rich archaeological record from the Dødemandsbugten site (Larsen 1934), from Kempe Fjord and Kong Oskar Fjord (Glob 1935), as well as from a smaller more recent excavation on Jameson Land in the Scoresby Sund Fjord system authorised by the Greenland

National Museum and Archives (Tuborg Sandell and Sandell 1991). In *Southeast Greenland*, only the Carlsberg Foundation Expedition (1898–1900) collected two bow fragments north of Ammassalik (Amdrup 1902).

The majority of bows and arrows originate from graves – especially in the Disko Bay – and from settlements. Seven bows and two arrows are classified as stray finds. Ethnographic objects come from the Thule district and Nuuk Fjord. For eight bows and 17 arrows the context cannot be specified (Appendix A1 and 2).

The *ethnographic objects* were collected by contemporaries amongst a living population who made and used them in daily life (Grønnow 2010, 120; 126). If well preserved and documented, they can provide the most detailed information for a technological study as they still retain their original dimensions as well as components of fragile materials like skin, sinew and feathers. The Kunstkammer bow (Pl. 1: Lb. 1) and the arrow Lc. 32b from Nuuk Fjord, both brought back to Denmark by one of the first European expeditions to West Greenland in the 17th century (Gundestrup 1991, 273), are outstanding examples of authentic hunting weapons used during the big caribou summer hunts in that region. In Trondheim (Norway), there is even a complete archery set collected by missionaries in the same region during the 18th century, consisting of bow and arrows, a quiver-bow case combination of seal skin with an ivory handle, and an attached pouch with tools (NTNU Vitenskapsmuseet 2008, 52; 62; 63). Although it is very likely that this set was assembled from objects that did not originally belong together, they are all nevertheless witnesses to the golden age of the West Greenland bow. Also of great importance in this context are two early and richly detailed oil paintings depicting Greenlanders from the Nuuk Fjord system with their hunting equipment, by an anonymous artist from Bergen (dated 1654) and by B. Grodtschilling (dated 1724) (Gulløv 1997, 355 ff.; Gundestrup 1991, 84 f.) (Pl. 31 and 32). Yet, there are some ethnographic specimens that also originate from a living population, but whose authenticity as functional hunting weapons must be evaluated very critically. To this group belong all the examined specimens from the Thule region (Plates 4–8), which are in fact models made for researchers to illustrate the technique at the beginning of the 20th century – at a time when the weapon had already disappeared from practical use (Birket-Smith 1918, 4; Steensby 1910, 157; Thomsen 1928, 320). Another example of such "secondary" ethnographic objects are the bow and arrows L 17.88 and L 17.89 (Pl. 9) which according to the museum records were found by Polar Greenlanders during a hunting trip to Ellesmere Island, very likely in a grave, brought back home to Uummannaq and then equipped with a new cable backing and partially new shafts and arrowheads according to their ideas of what they should have looked like. The whole set was then sold to inspector H. Nielsen in 1938 and eventually found its way into the collections of the National Museum of Denmark. A very critical early comment concerning the value of such doubtlessly very interesting specimens for technological studies is made by Steensby referencing the above-mentioned bows from Thule (1910, 357 f.):

"It appeared however, in the first place, that Masaitsiak [the maker] was quite aware, that these bows and arrows were not made really for caribou hunting, but only to satisfy the odd whims of the strangers, so that they did not require to be exactly right (...). We have here a problem, the solution of which would be of greatest ethnographic interest. How many pieces do the ethnographic collections not contain, which would prove to be quite valueless types if we knew exactly their previous history?"

Most of the *grave finds* were collected in the Disko Bay area during the long-term activities of Danish officials like inspector Krarup-Smith and the medic Dr Pfaff in the second half of the 19th century. Generally, these objects are in very good condition, often retaining their original smooth surfaces and dimensions (Pl. 1: Lb. 194). In some cases, especially on the baleen bows, parts are weathered (away) (Pl. 1: L. 5658). Others are partially eaten by invertebrates, very likely not *in situ* but during their first years in private collections (Pl. 1: Lb. 190 and Lb. 232). Features of hide, sinew, and feathers are only very rarely preserved (Pl. 1: Lb. 194 and L. 1958.2). Yet, their former presence can still frequently be deduced from indentations or shadows on the wood (Pl. 1: Lb. 430d).

The finds from Thule culture *settlements*, i.e. campsites, tent rings, house ruins and middens, unsurprisingly represent the biggest group. One source are the numerous archaeological excavations which frequently yielded stratigraphies, rendering a relative and sometimes absolute chronology possible (Gulløv 1997, 434). Another category, especially from East Greenland (Grønnow 2010, 122; 127), are un-stratified surface finds accompanying settlement structures. The preservation of the settlement finds is consequently very heterogeneous. While the archaeological objects often are reworked and highly fragmented but in overall good condition due to the favourable organic preservation in the permafrozen sediment (Pl. 1: L 6.884; 23), the surface finds are typically large pieces being more or less severely weathered and often overgrown by lichen (comp. Pfeifer 2014, 19 f.) (Pl. 1: L 1.4401). Despite some deformation (Pl. 18: Lc. 81; 26: L 1.4293), their original shape and dimensions can nevertheless be reconstructed in most cases.

That also applies to the last group, the *stray finds* that according to the records were collected from the surface without any associated structures. As the recent discoveries from Canadian and Norwegian ice patches show, arrows were regularly lost during hunting activities far away from settlements (Alix et al. 2012; Farbregd 2009) (Pl. 1: L 1.6657). This is, however, rather difficult to imagine for the seven bows attributed to that category. Most, if not all, Greenlandic Thule bows classified as stray finds in the museum records probably originally belonged to a settlement context – a tent ring or house for instance –

or a grave. These structures were simply not preserved or recognised (comp. Grønnow 2010, 127).

It is of note that all arrows included in this study are true individuals. In the global ethnographic record the arrows of a functional set tend to be similar in regard to mass, shape of nock and fletching, and active shaft length to ensure identical ballistic behaviour (Cattelain 1997; Roth 2004; Rots and Lepers 2020). Of course, uniformity is less important if the shooting distance is short. But even the arrow sets of 19th century Native American societies from the Great Plains who used to ride up to buffalo at point-blank range before shooting are usually very standardised (Bohr 2000, 45 f.) Thus, the lack of obvious arrow sets from Greenland is very likely a result of find context (Map 2): Arrows recovered from settlement middens or lost during the hunt are always single pieces (comp. Alix et al. 2012, fig. 2 and 3), and in graves usually just one or two arrows were added *pars pro toto* (e.g. Glob 1935, fig. 37; Larsen 1934, fig. 22). Possible arrow sets from West Greenland are nevertheless represented by Lb. 430a–d, L. 2879a and b, L. 2878c–e and L. 2878a and b (Pl. 22).

3.2. Analysis

3.2.1. Raw materials (Map 3; Appendix A3 and 7)

The majority of Greenland bow staves are made of Siberian conifer driftwood from pine, spruce or larch. To differentiate between these species was not possible without taking samples though (cf. Alix 2009, 153; Grønnow 1996, 83). Leafed trees, like birch or willow, were never worked. According to the ethno-historic information provided by O. Fabricius (1818, 236) and S. Kleinschmidt (1871), the strongly preferred material for bow making in West Greenland was a fine-grained coniferous wood with a reddish colour called *ikkeq*. The associated tree species is possibly larch (Grønnow 1996, 80; Walls 2010, tab 1). *Ikkeq* is said to be heavy, hard and pliable, and it takes a very smooth surface when worked (Grønnow et al. 1983, 27; Grønnow 1996, 80; Petersen 1986, 18) – all typical characteristics of good bow wood (Baker 1991, 104). Indeed, many of the well-preserved Greenlandic wood bow staves appear very dense, shiny and heavy. That raises a question: How can conifer wood being comparatively stiff, soft, and lightweight (Alix et al. 2012; Baker 1991, 105), have such properties?

Regardless of the species, the strength of wood is basically determined by its lignin content. The higher the percentage of lignin the stronger the wood. In conifers, a high lignin content is provided by narrow growth rings (Alix et al. 2021; Baker 1991, 102). For that reason, e.g. good yew

wood bows have to be fine-ringed (Hardy 2006, 203). However, according to the number of growth rings in the Greenland conifer wood bows (Tab. 1) it can be stated that the raw material is not particularly fine-ringed, even less so by Arctic standards (comp. Alix 2001; 2009; Alix et al. 2012). The solution to that paradox would be that a special kind of conifer wood was used: compression wood (Insulander 1999; Lepola 2015). Conifers build up compression wood on the lower side of horizontal branches and on the downhill side of trunks growing on slopes to counteract gravity. Compression wood is very rich in lignin and therefore much darker, harder and stronger than the rest of the tree, even within the same growth ring. When worked it has a typical shiny, glassy appearance and the growth rings are comparatively broad (Insulander 2002, 67). Compression wood was the material of choice for the laminated wood bows of the North European Saami and medieval Norwegians and was also used by different Siberian ethnicities (Insulander 2002; Lepola 2015). Lepola (2015, 55) states the use of compression wood of black spruce in wood-based composites by the Copper Inuit, who called it *itkiq*. In all likelihood, the Greenland wood bow stave was made of compression wood as well. The ethnographic information on the properties of *ikkeq* further supports that notion in stating that it originates from the outer layers of the log (Grønnow 1996, 80) and is curved towards its core (Grønnow et al. 1983; Fienup-Riordan 2007, 61). This exactly applies for a plank of compression wood taken from a bent branch or log. *Ikkeq* is definitely not the regular heartwood of the conifer tree (which is called *piqqeq*), being more reddish in colour and less pliable (Petersen 1986, 18). Yet, most convincing is the meaning of *ikkeq* in Alaskan Kobuk language: "irregular hard section in the tree rings" (Petersen 1986, 18; Webster and Zibell 1970). That is exactly what compression wood is. Compression wood can be found in all conifer species and is not restricted to larch. However, the extensive Greenlandic wood vocabulary is not so much about the exact botanical species, but rather about different properties and workability. (Alix 2009; Petersen 1986, 18 ff.).

In most cases, the growth rings lie horizontally within the bow limb (Tab. 2; Pl. 2 and 20):

Compared to a vertical or diagonal orientation, horizontal rings are reported to make a slightly more flexible limb (Baker 1993, 34). Frequently, somewhat twisted wood was used for the bow stave, resulting in one limb with a horizontal and the other with a diagonal growth ring orientation (Pl. 20: Lb. 232; 21: Lb. 1). In some cases the bow stave is constructed of wood with a thin strip of baleen on the back (Pl. 3: Lb. 1). From a technological point of

Tab. 1 Number of growth rings in Greenland wooden bow staves in the National Museum of Denmark (N = 23)

Growth rings per cm	4–6	7–9	10–12	13–15	16–18	19–21
N	7	6	4	2	3	1

Tab. 2 Orientation of the growth rings in wooden bow staves from Greenland (N = 30)

Growth ring orientation	horizontal	vertical	diagonal
N	16	4	10

view, one would rather expect to find the baleen on the belly to handle the compression strain. Yet, as baleen is also very tension strong it could be used as a transitional layer between cable backing and wooden stave. The visual complexity and appeal of the different combined layers might also have played a role. Laminated composites of baleen and spliced composites of caribou antler (Pl. 4 and 11) are strongly linked to regions where either driftwood is very scarce or extensive whale hunting took place: Polar and Northwest as well as Northeast Greenland (Birket-Smith 1918, 13; Thomsen 1928, 320) (Tab. 3; Map 3 and 4).

For the cable backing, plaited sinew or hide thongs were used (Fig. 2.6). In a specimen of the Arctic type, the lower layer is made from hide and the upper from sinew (Pl. 21). If there are wrappings to fix the cable to the bow stave, the prevailing materials are hide and occasionally sinew (Pl. 1 and 5). Both twisted hide and sinew were used for the bow string (Pl. 5).

Every single studied arrow shaft from Greenland is made from conifer wood and, contrary to the bows, very often from pieces with a relatively high percentage of early growth wood (Pl. 24). Conifer wood is a good material for arrow shafts because it is stiff and can easily be split from logs in straight pieces. Due to its rather low hardness and regular grain it is also easily worked (Beckhoff 1965). Not surprisingly, many hunting arrow shafts from the ice patches in the Canadian Subarctic and virtually all from High Arctic Canadian sites attributed to the Thule culture are made from conifer wood (Alix 2001; Alix et al. 2012). With a few exceptions, the foreshafts and points are of caribou antler: Antler arrowheads are hard, stiff and tough and can therefore absorb a great amount of energy when

hitting hard objects like bones, gravel or frozen soil. Yet, smaller damages can easily be repaired. Furthermore, the material is heavy, giving a good impact. Again in the Canadian ice patches, caribou antler is well represented in foreshafts and points of darts and arrows (Hare 2004). Wrappings for fastening arrowhead and fletching as well as for the nock reinforcement are always of sinew because of its strength (Pl. 3). It also shrinks as it dries, enhancing the stability of the wrapping even more. Sometimes traces of a dark substance can be observed which could be blood glue (comp. Balikci 1989, 19) (Pl. 24: L. 2878b).

3.2.2. Design (Appendix A5 and 9)

Bow cross sections

There are three different limb cross sections (Map 5). The rectangular cross section with a flat back and a slightly rounded belly is the prevailing one. It evenly distributes the tension and compression forces over the whole surface of back and belly, thus providing the toughest possible design for a bow limb (Baker 1992, 63; Junkmanns 2013, 55). The d-shaped cross section also distributes the tension load over the whole back of the limb but concentrates the compression forces on a relatively narrow strip on the belly. Therefore, a d-cross section requires materials that are very strong in compression and/or a comparatively greater bow length to avoid cell collapse (Baker 1992, 63). Good examples of that design option are medieval yew longbows from England and Scandinavia (Hardy 2006, 212; 214; Paulsen 1999). Compared to the rectangular form, a d-cross section of the same thickness and hence bending strength is lighter, and it is also more convenient to make as the blade of the cutting tool always rests only on a small surface (Baker 1994, 58 f.). A triangular cross section is found to be still more effective as it is even lighter (Riesch 2002, 22) but the risk of failure increases dramatically as a narrow keel has to take the bulk of the compression load (Junkmanns 2013, 348). Additionally, it is very time consuming to manufacture. The triangular cross section is found on only one specimen (Pl. 18 and 20: Lc. 81).

Tab. 3 Selected measurements (in cm) of baleen bows from Greenland

Inv.-number	Bow length	Width mid-limb	Thickness mid-limb	Width tip	Thickness tip
Northwest Greenland					
A.2.c.4	104 (reconstructed)	3.3	1.8	3.3	0.9
L. 5658	> 110	3.2	no inf.	3.1	no inf.
L. 7861	82.1	2.5	1.4	2.3	0.7
Lc. 356	118	3.3	1.7	2.8	1
L 6.781	no inf.	no inf.	no inf.	> 2	1
Northeast Greenland					
L. 3327	no inf.	no inf.	no inf.	2.4	no inf.
Southeast Greenland					
L. 6615	no inf.	no inf.	no inf.	2.5	no inf.

Tab. 4 Selected measurements (in cm) of Greenland Thule culture bows with wooden staves

Inv.-number	Bow length	Width mid-limb	Thickness mid-limb	Width tip	Thickness tip	Reference
Northwest Greenland						
L. 2881	97.6	3.3	1.4	2.9	1.1	this study
L. 4569	112	3.5	1.3	no inf.	no inf.	this study
L. 4568	118	3.4	1.5	2.7	1.4	this study
L. 1957	121	no inf.	no inf.	no inf.	no inf.	Birket-Smith 1918
L. 8857	105	4	no inf.	2.5	no inf.	Birket-Smith 1918
Central West Greenland						
L 6.884	no inf.	no inf.	no inf.	> 3	1.4	this study
L 6.685	no inf.	no inf.	no inf.	3	1.6	this study
L. 4386	143	no inf.	no inf.	no inf.	no inf.	Birket-Smith 1918
L. 4817	142	no inf.	no inf.	no inf.	no inf.	Birket-Smith 1918
L. 8565	> 125	no inf.	no inf.	no inf.	no inf.	Birket-Smith 1918
Lb. 1	136	3.7	1.6	3.2	1.4	this study
Lb. 35	159	3.8	2.3	3.3	1.8	this study
Lb. 134	134	no inf.	no inf.	no inf.	no inf.	Birket-Smith 1918
Lb. 190	ca. 140	3.3	1.5	no inf.	no inf.	this study
Lb. 194	134	3.3	1.7	3.1	1.3	this study
Lb. 232	128	3.5	1.3	2.6	1.4	this study
Lb. 233	> 150	3.4	1.9	3.3	2	this study
Lc. 81	148	4.3	1.8	> 3	1.7	this study
Lc. 365	142	no inf.	no inf.	no inf.	no inf.	Birket-Smith 1918
igd 3352	no inf.	no inf.	no inf.	3	1.6	Gulløv 1997
Bergen painting 1654	more than waist-high	no inf.	no inf.	no inf.	no inf.	this study
Copenhagen painting 1724	shoulder high	no inf.	no inf.	no inf.	no inf.	this study
Northeast Greenland						
Lc. 1424	150	3.9	1.5	3.6	2.2	this study
Cambridge Exp.	no inf.	3.8	no inf.	no inf.	no inf.	Mathiassen 1929
Cambridge Exp.	no inf.	3.5	no inf.	no inf.	no inf.	Mathiassen 1929
KNK 566	ca. 130	4	no inf.	4	2.2	Tuborg Sandell and Sandell 1991
Nathorst Exp.	ca. 130	no inf.	no inf.	no inf.	no inf.	Nathorst 1900
Bartlett Exp.	114	no inf.	no inf.	no inf.	no inf.	Bartlett 1931
Bartlett Exp.	156	no inf.	no inf.	no inf.	no inf.	Bartlett 1931
Richter Exp.	> 120	3	1.8	4.5	2	Richter 1934
Norwegian hunters' find	134	no inf.	no inf.	no inf.	no inf.	Richter 1934
Schwach's find	> 130	3.6	1.5	4	2.3	this study
L 1.3527	> 110	3.6	1.4	4	1.9	this study
L. 1.3867	no inf.	no inf.	no inf.	3.6	1.7	this study
L. 1.4293	107	3.4	1.1	2.4	1.5	this study
L. 3660	> 110	2.8	1.2	no inf.	no inf.	this study
L. 3862	> 120	3.5	1.4	no inf.	no inf.	this study
L 1.4401	> 130	3.7	1.2	3.9	1.9	this study
L. 3661	> 120	3.4	1.4	no inf.	no inf.	this study
L 1.4183	> 120	4	1.5	3.5	1.5	this study
Dødemandsbugten – Grave 6	no inf.	3.6	no inf.	no inf.	no inf.	Larsen 1934
Dødemandsbugten – No. 2582	> 120	no inf.	no inf.	4.2	2	Larsen 1934
Southeast Greenland						
L. 6617	> 120	3.4	1.7	no inf.	no inf.	this study

Bow silhouettes, limb taper and profiles

The silhouette most often seen on the Greenland bow is a paddle-shaped one with the widest point being at mid-limb and narrowing in gently curved lines towards the tips, which are slightly widened again. Other bows have more or less straight sides, sometimes with slight contractions at mid-limb. The handle section is almost always narrowed (Pl. 4; 10; 11; 18; 19; 26; 27). Narrow grips favour both grip comfort and flight behaviour of the arrow, as it can leave the bow almost in a straight line and does not have to wind around the bow so much – a phenomenon known as *archer's paradox* (Klopsteg 1947). The generally wide and thick tips are heavy and therefore mechanically inefficient (Tab. 4). However, as they have to hold not only the string but also the cable backing, they must be wide and also stable enough.

In the examples of bows with a simple d-profile (Fig. 2.3), the tapering of the limbs indicates that they all worked over their entire length, including the narrowed handle section. The tips are thickened and therefore, stiff (Tab. 4; Pl. 18 and 19). To make a narrow handle that bends is deemed to be very challenging by modern bowyers as it must be thin enough to bend but rigid enough not to bend too much (Baker 1992, 55). Most of the bow's bending is distributed over its wide and flat mid-limb portions, which is energy efficient because they are relatively short and therefore, light (Baker 1994, 50). The stiff tips, again, keep the string angle low and hence counteract stacking (see above). To conclude, contrary to their plain appearance, the wooden d-bows from Greenland were sophisticated and highly optimised designs. The double-curved antler composites from Polar Greenland (Pl. 4) owing to their elastic splint joints (Boas 1907, 394) probably also worked throughout their entire length. However, as the string angle at the tips is comparatively high by default in such a design (Baker 1994, 64; Hamilton 1982) and because of the very short bow and draw length, energy storage can be expected to be rather low. Frequently, the double-curved bows are asymmetric with the upper limb being both longer and more curved than the lower. Both double-curved profile and asymmetry are also typical for many North American Plains bows from the 19th century (Allely and Hamm 2002), and there are lively debates about the pros and cons of this design (Hamilton 1982, 44 ff.; Koppedrayer 2004). One argument brought forth is that asymmetric bows give the arrow a flatter trajectory (Bohr 1998, 49). Concerning the particular case of Greenland antler bows, the double-curved profile is probably best explained with the shape of the raw material: Antler segments are always curved and when joining three of them to a bow stave, the double curved profile suggests itself as the most convenient and stable design. The recurved bow is represented by only one baleen fragment, most probably one layer of the limb of a laminated composite (Pl. 10: L. 5658). If reconstructed with a working handle and long, stiff recurves (Grayson 1993, 134; 149), this would have been a high energy storing bow (comp. Baker 1992, 57). In the triple-curved bow, the bending is distributed over one big circle segment at the middle and two smaller ones at the ends. The angular transitional zones between the bends are always thickened or supported by bracers and therefore, rigid (Pl. 21 and 27). As there are no experimental data such as shooting distances or f-d curves available, that design is difficult to judge. The often quite pronounced backward angulation of the rear curves in relaxed position (Pl. 11) would result in a beneficial high early draw weight. Yet, their bending action later in the draw produces a fairly high string angle (comp. Pl. 37) making that design presumably less energy-storing than a recurve. The triple-curved bow was doubtlessly the most elaborate and challenging design to make. However, its wide distribution all over the North American Arctic (Murdoch 1890) suggests that it must have had some benefits over other designs, or at least no drawbacks.

Regardless of their profile, all Greenland bows must originally have been reflexed to a certain degree when unstrung owing to the tension of the strong cable backing (Pl. 18: Lb. 194; 19: Lb. 35). This benefits energy storage because early draw weight is higher than in straight or even deflex staves.

Arrow design

The arrow shafts of the Greenland Thule culture are typically tapered, being thickest at the distal and getting progressively thinner towards the proximal end or, barrelled, being thickest at about mid-shaft and tapering towards either end (comp. Alix et al. 2012, 106; Junkmanns 2013, 400). Cylindrical shafts are only rarely found. The proximal end is almost always flattened and the nock section is broadened (Pl. 6; 14; 15; 22; 23; 29). The flattened proximal end and nock make the draw more comfortable than if left round: Short bows with relatively long draw lengths result in low string angles at the arrow nock that can pinch the fingers quite severely when the so-called 'Mediterranean release' with the index finger above and the middle finger below the nock is used. Flattening the nock counteracts this tendency. Another benefit of the arrow's flattened proximal end is that it provides a favourable contact surface for the tangential fletching which is the single most important method encountered in Greenland. A flattened proximal section and widened nock are also very typical for Thule culture arrows from the Canadian Arctic (Alix 2001). The very common lanceolate silhouette of the arrowheads has proven to be a good compromise for both cutting and piercing (Miller et al. 1986, 190). Heavy osseous arrowheads on light wooden shafts result in a balance point located well in the front third of the arrow. Though not favouring a long flight (Lepers and Rots 2020, 4), a forward point of balance quickly stabilises the arrow's trajectory. With its flattened end and tangential fletching, the Greenland arrow is clearly not axially symmetric. High-speed filming would reveal how much it actually rotates during its flight. Notably, there is a clear design parallel to the Greenland winged harpoon which is reported to merely 'glide' through the water (Petersen 1986, 79; Gulløv 2005, 311).

3.2.3. Technology (Appendix A6 and 10)

Treatment of the grain

Wood is composed of tightly packed longitudinally running fibre bundles. For maximum tension strength, the grain should not be violated (Baker 1993, 35). This is traditionally accomplished by working the back of the bow to one growth ring as well as by following the lateral fibre path. If not using wood from an unusually large, straight, and branchless trunk, the bow will consequently display some bumps and curves, and its back will be more or less rounded, progressively more the wider it is (Baker 1992, 64). Iron Age and Medieval yew longbows with their often quite rustic appearance are prominent examples of this technological concept (Junkmanns 2013, fig. 236; 271; pl. 96; 99; 101; Paulsen 1999). The Greenland Thule bowyers, in stark contrast, always went for an absolutely flat back and wanted their bows to be as even and symmetrical as possible. Therefore, they inevitably had to cut through growth rings and also to violate the grain, but they knew precisely to what degree the material would tolerate that (Pl. 2). There are only three examples displaying the typical transversal cracks on the back indicative of tension failure (comp. Baker 1992, 103) (Pl. 27 and 28: Schwach's find and L 1.4401; 12: L. 4568b). In some cases (Pl. 2 and 18: Lc. 81), the bow staves from smaller diameter logs are de-crowned (Baker 1993, 27), meaning that the severely curved growth rings on the back were cut through to flatten it while staying parallel with the overall fibre path. One bow shows reversely running growth rings and the pith groove on the back (Pl. 2 and 20: Lb. 194) clearly indicating that the inner part of the small log/branch made the back and the outer rings the belly. Such 'backward' bows have once been postulated for the European Neolithic (e.g. Comstock 1993 b, 91) but were finally rejected based on closer analyses of the archaeological finds and because of technological reasons (Junkmanns 2013, 1 f.) Yet, as conifer compression wood is built up mainly on the outer part of the log, bow staves from that particular raw material can very well be oriented 'backward' (comp. Lepola 2015).

When working antler and baleen, the grain is naturally largely followed because the pre-forms are elongated and flattish to start with. In lateral barbs on antler arrowheads, however, the longitudinal grain is inevitably violated (Pl. 25). The high splitting resistance of the material renders that possible though (Margaris 2014).

Splices and joining techniques

Whenever a wooden composite bow stave had to be assembled, the v-scarf (Fig. 2.5) was used (Birket-Smith 1918, 17; Holtved 1944, pl. 10,17–19; Mathiassen 1930, 194; pl. 6,17; Mathiassen 1931, 81; Porsild 1915a, fig. 20) (Pl. 3: L 1.4293). The oblique scarf, which is common in other Eastern Arctic bow making traditions (Birket-Smith 1945, 53; Jenness 1946, 122; Mathiassen 1945, 55 f.), is never found in Greenland. In antler composites, only the

splinting technique was applied (Pl. 3: Lu. 324). Baleen bow staves, again, were always built up of horizontally overlapping layers (Pl. 11). It becomes obvious that there is a strict connection between raw material and the chosen joining technique. The v-scarf is fixed by wrappings and reinforced by bracers on the back side (Glob 1934–37, 78; fig. 37g; Mathiassen 1930, 194; 1934, 97; pl. 16,17; Mathiassen 1934, 97). In the splint joint, the meeting ends are sewn together and then the bracers wrapped on (Birket-Smith 1918, fig. 1d) (Pl. 3: Lu. 324 and L. 17.88). The laminations of baleen bows are sewn together as well (Pl. 3: Lc. 356). In bows with a single baleen strip as back reinforcement, the back of the wooden main stave is sometimes cut out to receive it. Apart from that, it is mainly the pressure of the cable backing that holds it in place (Pl. 3: Lb. 1 and Lc. 1424). The arrows of the Greenland Thule culture feature screwing, splitting, and scarfing in order to join arrowhead and wooden main shaft (Pl. 3). The fixing is achieved by means of wrappings. Iron points were riveted to the osseous foreshafts (Pl. 3: Lu. 327b).

3.3. Regional Variability

3.3.1. Polar Greenland (Pl. 4–9)

Typical for both the Thule region and Inglefield Land are spliced composites of wood or caribou antler (Map 3 and 4). In some cases, baleen was used (Holtved 1944, 211). Wrapped-on bracers of antler or tusk for reinforcing the splices are very common (Holtved 1944, pl. 10,21–23; Malaurie 1990, 184; Steensby 1910, 354). With lengths ranging from 75–90 cm, the Polar antler bows are by far the shortest in Greenland (Pl. 4; Appendix A4). Doubtlessly, the dimensions of the available raw materials account for that. If the models from the beginning of the 20th century are vaguely correct (see 3.1.), these antler bows have a double-curved, asymmetrical profile with the upper limb being both slightly longer and also more curved than the lower (Malaurie 1990, 184). The cross section is d-shaped or rectangular (Pl. 4; Map. 5). While the d-cross section is functional because it respects the structure of the raw material by allowing the tough antler compacta to form the belly of the bow (Pl. 4: L. 10300 and L 17.111), the rectangular one is mostly week spongiosa and thus of very limited practical use (Pl. 5: x. 174, Lu. 323 and Lu. 324). It appears that the makers of these specimens either had already lost some knowledge of how to make a functional antler bow or they simply did not bother because they were just producing models for ethnographers (comp. Steensby 1910, 357). The Polar Greenland bows always have an Eastern cable backing consisting of one single layer of strands stretching from nock to nock (Fig. 2.6). Judging by the studied objects it is not twisted (Pl. 5). Accordingly, only one single cable twister of wood is known from archaeological context (Holtved 1944, 212; pl. 10).

The ethnographic arrows from Polar Greenland have short main shafts with lengths of only 35–45 cm and flared proximal ends. The nocks are very broad and flat and the shallow string grooves are u or v-shaped. A heavy foreshaft of antler with a riveted iron point is most common. The joint between main shaft and arrowhead is often an oblique scarf wrapped with sinew. If the arrow has a point of iron, it is set into the split main shaft (Pl. 6 and 7; Appendix A 7–10). The overall rather rustic appearance of the Polar Greenland specimens most likely results from their model character, as an original arrow shaft from nearby Ellesmere Island is much more delicately executed (Pl. 9: L 17.89a). The frequent absence of fletching may be likewise explained – although there are several archaeological and ethnographic bow shooting traditions with un-fletched arrows (e.g. Lepers and Rots 2020; Tukura 1994). In the archaeological record from Thule district and Inglefield Land some tangentially fletched arrows are present and there is also broad evidence of lanceolate and barbed arrow points of antler and occasionally tusk with conical tangs set into closed sockets of the shaft (Holtved 1944, pl. 11; 12). Some archaeological arrow shafts are spliced together from several short pieces (Holtved 1944, pl. 12,8).

Bow and arrow were kept and carried together in a quiver-bow case combination of rawhide also comprising a pouch for tools (Malaurie 1990, 184) (Pl. 7 and 8). The wood, antler and ivory carrying handles are typical archaeological finds in Polar Greenland (Holtved 1944, pl. 12,12–21; 1954, 67).

3.3.2. Northwest Greenland (Pl. 10–17)

On Disko Island and along the Northwest coast, with lengths of 100–120 cm the bow is notably longer than in Polar Greenland (Appendix A4). Beside self bow staves (Pl. 10: L. 4568 and L. 2881) there are also wooden composites, assembled from three pieces (Mathiassen 1930, 194; pl. 6,17; Porsild 1915a, fig. 20) (Appendix A3 and A6; Pl. 10: L. 4569; Map 3 and 4). Mathiassen (1930, 194; 1934, 97; pl. 16,17) reports wooden or antler bracers for reinforcing the curved parts and splices on the bow's back from Inussuk site. The hypothesis of "separate antler end caps" (Mathiassen (1930, 194), however, cannot be assessed due to the lack of illustrations and detailed descriptions. The silhouettes of the bows are either straight-sided with only slightly narrowed handle sections, or paddle shaped with contractions at mid-limb (Appendix A5; Pl. 10). There are bows with a d-profile and a d-shaped cross section as well as triple-curved bows with a rectangular one (Map 5 and 6). The first group probably had a two-layer Arctic cable backing resting on shoulders (Fig. 2.6: L. 1957; Pl. 10 and 12: L. 2881). The latter (Pl. 10 and 12: L. 4568) could either have had an Arctic backing with the upper layer fixed at the mid-limb contractions or a one-layer Eastern backing stretching from nock to nock. The rather delicate bow tips (Tab. 4) speak for the Arctic type. On Uummannaq Peninsula, the laminated baleen composite was made (Mathiassen 1930, 194; pl. 21; 1934, 97; pl. 5,1) (Pl. 10: L. 5658; 11 and 13; Map 4). The toughness of the material facilitated a short, highly reflexed bow. The cross section is rectangular and the profile is triple-curved or, rarely, recurved. Only one specimen has distinct shoulders

for the Arctic backing (Pl. 10: L. 5658). The others have lateral rows of indentations at mid-limb (Pl. 11 and 13) – either for a two-layer Arctic backing or just for a strong wrapping to hold down an Eastern backing at the sharp angles. All evidence suggests that these delicately looking baleen bows were actually full-weight hunting weapons. Cable twisters and marline spikes of wood and antler for adjusting the cable backing, with or without a central hole, are well-attested at the archaeological site of Inussuk (Mathiassen 1930, 195; pl. 7,15.16).

There is only one arrow in the collections of the National Museum that can undoubtedly be attributed to this region. It is a grave find (Pl. 14: L. 1958.2), has a shaft length of only 45 cm and belongs to a 121 cm long bow (Fig. 2.6; Appendix A1: L. 1957). Some arrows from West Greenland with unclear provenance having short, sturdy shafts (Pl. 14: Lb. 116.1 and 2; Lb. 111a–c; 15: L. 2880a–e, Lb. 3) and forming a very homogenous and distinct metric group (Fig. 3.1) thus presumably originate from the northern part of Greenland's west coast. The shafts are tapered towards the proximal end and have a flattened and often broadened nock with a v-shaped string groove. The fletching is short and tangential (Pl. 16). Arrow points are always of caribou antler and have a lanceolate silhouette with two, one or without barbs and a biconvex, flattened diamond-shaped, or triangular cross section. The tang is usually long and has either two staggered knobs or a screw thread for inserting into a closed socket (Mathiassen 1930, 195; 1934, 97; Porsild 1915a, fig. 21) (Appendix A7–10). Plate 17 shows some examples from northwest Disko Island (Appendix A11). Composite arrowheads seem to be rare. The complete arrow from Uummannaq features an antler foreshaft with an iron point (Pl. 14: L. 1958.2). Further examples of foreshafts with metal points come from the archaeological site of Inussuk (Mathiassen 1930, pl. 7,21).

3.3.3. Central West Greenland (Pl. 18–25)

From southern Disko Bay down to Nuuk Fjord, a wooden self bow stave with a paddle shaped silhouette was characteristic (Pl. 18 and 19; Appendix A3–6). Additionally, there is evidence of the laminated composite bow: the Kunstkammer bow with a baleen strip applied to the back at mid-section (Pl. 19 and 21: Lb. 1) and the bow in the Bergen painting picturing a layer of dark material at the same position which, according to its colour, should also be baleen (Pl. 31). It is noteworthy that both examples come from the Nuuk Fjord. An Inuit informant from Aasiaat in the beginning of the 20th century also mentions a layer of 'whalebone' – probably baleen – applied to the back of the bow (Grønnow et al. 1983, 27). Besides some questionable fragments from Qeqertarmiut listed by Mathiassen (1931, 81), spliced composites were not produced in Central West Greenland as there was enough suitable driftwood for self bow staves (Map 3 and 4). Bow lengths range from 120 cm up to 160 cm, which would have been human high. Hence, the bow in Central West Greenland is considerably longer than in Northwest Greenland.

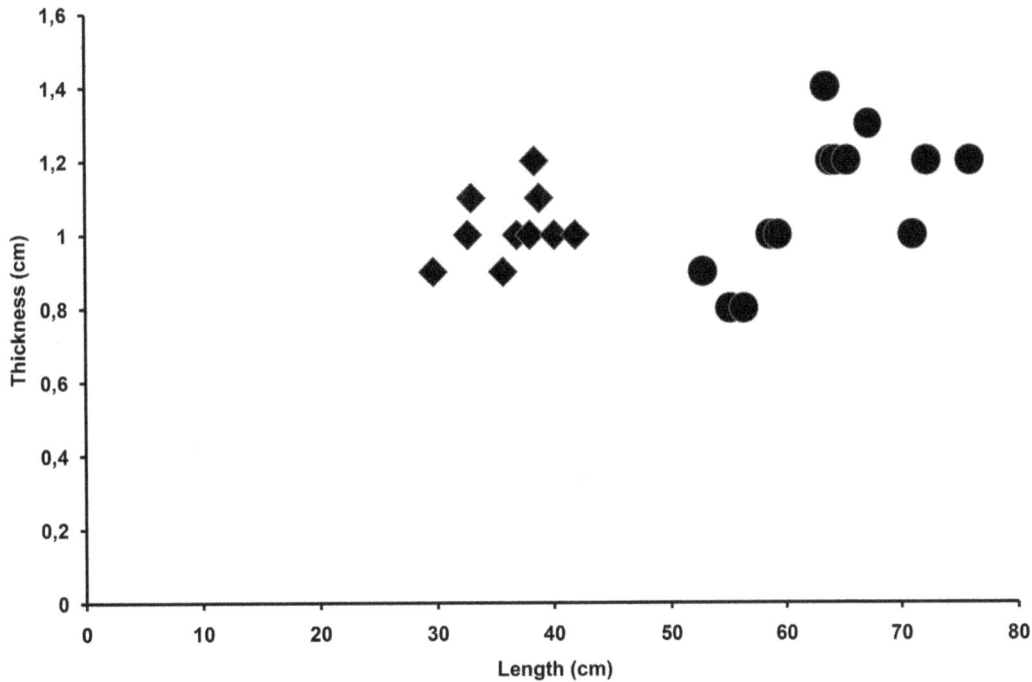

Fig. 3.1. Arrow shaft length and thickness. Diamond: presumably Northwest Greenland, dot: presumably Central West Greenland (N = 23).

Most bows have a simple d-profile with a working handle and a d-shaped cross section with a flat back and rounded belly (Pl. 18; 19; 20; Map 5 and 6). Yet, the Kunstkammer bow and a small bow from Qeqertarmiut (Pl. 30: L 12.1674) are triple-curved with the curves heat bent into the stave and supported by flat, angular wrapped-on antler bracers on the back (Pl. 21). Bracers of antler and wood are also present in the find material from Illutalik (Mathiassen 1934, 97) and Illorpaat (Gulløv 1997, 237). The triple-curved bows, as well as a d-bow from Aito in southern Disko Bay (Pl. 19 and 20: Lb. 190) have rectangular cross sections. The bows on the oil paintings from the 17th and 18th centuries (Pl. 31 and 32), the Kunstkammer bow (Pl. 21), a bow in the Greenland National Museum (Fig. 2.6: Lc. 365) and the Trondheim bow (NTNU Vitenskapsmuseet 2008, 62) are all equipped with the two-layer Arctic cable backing. Though no backing is preserved on the remaining specimens from Central West Greenland, the shallow shoulders every single specimen has at about mid-limb, frequently showing traces of the characteristic half-hitches (Pl. 20), strongly suggest that the Arctic backing type was generally applied. Cable twisters of wood, tusk and antler for adjusting the backing (Pl. 23: L. 2898) are well-represented at the archaeological sites of Illutalik (Mathiassen 1934, 7), Sermermiut (Mathiassen 1958, tab. 3), Qeqertarmiut (Mathiassen 1931, 81) and Kangeq (Gulløv 1997, 301). A whole set of twisters and marlin spikes from the 18th century, threaded on a thong, are kept at Trondheim (NTNU Vitenskapsmuseet 2008).

Like the bows, the arrows from Central West Greenland are generally quite long and sturdy (Fig. 3.1; Pl. 22; 23; Appendix A7–10). Shaft lengths ranging from 60 to 75 cm permitted a more or less full draw. The proximal end is flattened and flared and the string groove is most often u-shaped. In some cases, the nock is stepped (Pl. 22 and 24: L. 2878a and b). The fletching is tangential and judging by the traces of former wrappings sometimes very long, exceeding 20 cm (Pl. 22: L. 2878a–e). The long and massive antler arrow points with knob or screw tangs resemble the Northwest Greenland types (Mathiassen 1958, tab. 3) (Pl. 25). Additionally, antler foreshafts with long barbs and iron points are common (Mathiassen 1934, 97) (Pl. 23: L 6.876; 24: Lu. 704; 25). Some Inuit informants from the beginning of the 20th century state that this type was called *pangaligiaq* because of its ability to work itself further into a running animal, and also that it was meant to separate from the main shaft when the prey was hit (Grønnow et al. 1983, 29 f.) A barbed arrowhead working itself into the prey sounds quite odd. Nevertheless, the barbs surely prevented it from falling out again and also caused pain and hindered the animal's movements (Stefánsson 1914, 96). What is more, it was probably not intended that arrowhead and main shaft separated as a well balanced, straight arrow is very time consuming to make and an object of considerable value – especially in the Arctic. Among the Copper Inuit, for example, arrow shafts were used until totally worn (Stefánsson 1914, 96). Yet, it frequently happened incidentally that the shaft came off when the animal was hit with the usual result of a lost arrow (Stefánsson 1914, 92). Though the knob and screw tangs from Greenland are quite short, secured by a strong sinew wrapping they nevertheless can be expected to provide a durable and permanent joint.

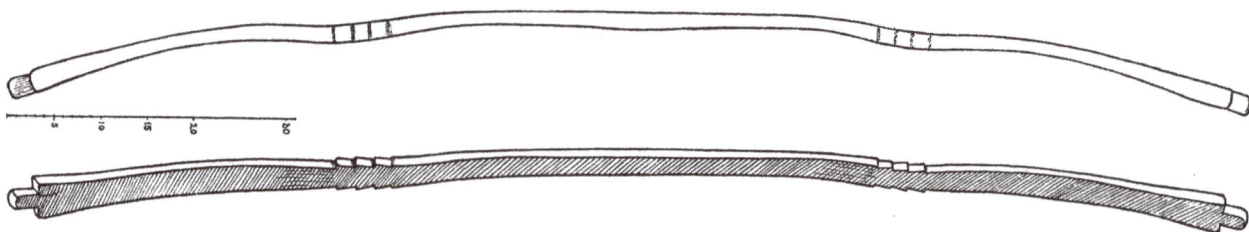

Fig. 3.2 Self bow stave found by Norwegian hunters on Gauss Halvø. Length 134 cm (Richter 1934, fig. 3.13,1).

In Trondheim, a typical Arctic quiver-bow case combination of waterproof sealskin with ivory handle and attached pouch is kept that was collected in the Nuuk Fjord in the 18th century (NTNU Vitenskapsmuseet 2008, 63).

Thanks to the ethnographic works of Fabricius (1818, 234 ff.), we know the Central West Greenlandic terms for archery equipment (modern West Greenlandic spelling in brackets, translation Nuka K. Godfredsen):

- whole archery set: *Pissiksisak*
- quiver-bow case combination: *Pôktak (Poortaq)*
- quiver: *Karksum Inna*; bow case: *Pissiksim Inna*; bag: *Takoarbik*
- bow: *Pissikse (Pisisseq)*
- bow stave: *Pissiksib Kerssukta*
- nock: *Nokarsarbik*
- bow string: *Nokartak (Noqartaq)*
- cable backing: *Kyak (Kiaq)*
- arrow: *Karksok (Qarsoq)*
- shaft: *Karksub Kerssukta*
- nock: *Erka (Ikka)*
- fletching: *Sulluee (Sulluii)*
- arrowhead: *Nàkok (Naqqoq), Ullunga (Ulunga)*
- barbs: *Akingee (Akingii)*
- wrappings: *Nervngee (Nerngii)*

3.3.4. East Greenland (Pl. 26–29)

From Nordostrundingen down to Scoresby Sound, the bow was widely used for caribou and musk ox hunting from the 15th until the beginning of the 19th century (Birket-Smith, 10; Grønnow and Jensen 2003, 340; Knuth 1981). Very limited evidence comes from southeast Greenland where the bow was unknown when the first Europeans arrived (Birket-Smith 1918, 6) (Map 1). Like its counterpart in Central West Greenland, the East Greenland bow is a full-draw weapon designed to cast heavy hunting arrows. Despite that, it shows marked differences in design and technology (Appendix A3–6).

The East Greenland bow is – with only two sure exceptions of self bows (Bartlett 1931, fig. 17) (Fig. 3.2) – a spliced wooden composite (Map 3 and 4), assembled from at least two pieces by means of 7–12 cm long v-scarfs that are reinforced by wrappings the indentations of which can occasionally be observed (Pl. 26 and 27). Several baleen bow tips from the Dødemandsbugten site (Larsen 1934,

105 f.; pl. 9,1) and two fragments from Maroussia and Southeast Greenland (Tab. 3), respectively, match the dimensions of complete Northwest Greenland specimens and can therefore be interpreted as parts of full-weight hunting weapons. Other baleen bows from East Greenland (e.g. Pl. 30: L. 3439) according to their dimensions are not suitable for big game hunting. Thomsen (1917, 400) interprets a bow found by Ryder (1895, fig. 2.7) as laminated from wood and a thin strip of baleen similar to the Kunstkammer bow from Central West Greenland. The piece in question (Pl. 3 and 26: Lc. 1424) indeed has a recess on the back which probably accommodated a now lost baleen strip.

The spliced-in end pieces resemble abstracted human figures with head, shoulders and legs (Pl. 27: L 1.3527 and L 1.4183; 28: L. 4058). In the Disko Bay area, such wooden bow tips hence were called *inûssâ* – translated by Porsild (1915a, 160) as 'its doll' or 'its man-likeness'. Doubtlessly, their shape is first of all determined by the functional requirements of holding both cable backing and bow string and providing a stable splice to the main stave. Yet, there is an example of a tip whose resemblance to a human head was accentuated by carving (Pl. 28: L 1.3867).

There is frequent evidence of wood and antler bracers, thick in the middle and tapering towards the ends, supporting the bow at the curves like in West Greenland (Bartlett 1931, fig. 17; Larsen 1934, 80; pl. 1,7; 12,14) (Fig. 3.3g). For accommodating them, the back of the bow is cut out in these places (Pl. 26).

However, many bows, especially the larger ones (Fig. 3.2; Pl. 27: Schwach's find and L 1.4401) (Nathorst 1900, 345; Richter 1934, fig. 2.52,1), do not have bracers but instead are left thicker at the bends. With few exceptions, the East Greenland bow is long, measuring around 130 cm and occasionally more (Bartlett 1931, fig. 17; Nathorst 1900, 345; Tuborg Sandell and Sandell 1991, 48) (Tab. 4; Fig. 3.2), and it is without exception triple-curved (Pl. 26 and 27; Map 6). Unlike in the West Greenlandic examples with that profile, the shallow curves were not heat bent into the wood but instead, as growth ring orientation and fibre path clearly show (Pl. 26: Lc. 1424; 27: Schwach's find and L 1.4401), were carved out of the full material. The limb taper of some specimens indicates a stiff handle section (Pl. 26: L. 3862) while others have a working one (Pl. 26: Lc. 1424). The silhouette is either paddle shaped with a

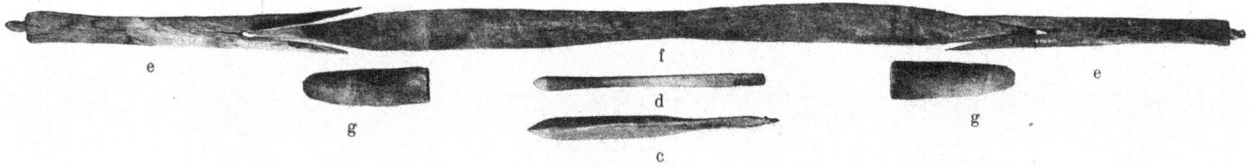

Fig. 3.3 Grave find L 1.4293 from Suess Land with wooden bracers and two arrowheads. Length of bow 107 cm (Glob 1935, fig. 37). Reproduced courtesy of Lotte and Anders Glob.

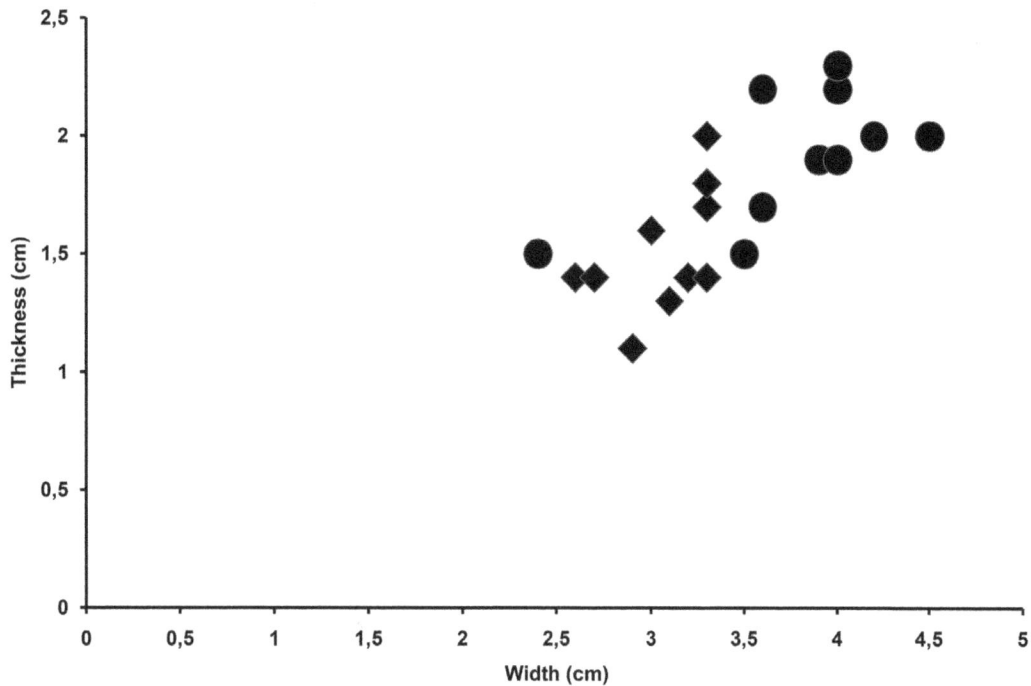

Fig. 3.4. Width and thickness of Greenland wood bow tips. Diamond: West Greenland, dot: East Greenland (N = 20).

gentle contraction at mid-limb (Pl. 26: Lc. 1424), or nearly straight-sided (Pl. 27: Schwach's find). The cross section is in any case rectangular with a flat back and an ever so slightly rounded belly (Pl. 26 and 27; Map 5).

There is not a single East Greenland bow with preserved cable backing. The absence of shoulders like on the West Greenland bows and the comparatively thick and wide nocks (Fig. 3.4) speak for the one-layered Eastern cable type as found on a tiny but very detailed bow model from a grave on Gauss Peninsula (Fig. 3.5). Some specimens have three pairs of lateral notches cut into the wood at both ends of the main bend (Richter 1934, fig. 2.52,1; Tuborg Sandell and Sandell 1991, fig. 23) (Pl. 27 and 28: Schwach's find and L 1.4401), supposedly to tie the backing cable down to the bow's back at the curved spots by means of a strong wrapping. This technique is also applied on the bows of the Copper Inuit (Damas 1984, fig. 3.2), Netsilik (Taylor 1974, pl. 8) and in Alaska (Murdoch 1890, pl. III). Its triple curved profile and spliced stave are other features that link the East Greenland composite to the bow making traditions of the Central Arctic.

Ivory cable twisters and marlin spikes are known from several archaeological sites in Northeast Greenland (Glob 1935, 50; pl. 6,26; Larsen 1934, pl. 4,12; Richter 1934, 122; Ryder 1895, fig. 3.4; Thomsen 1917, 402 f.; Tuborg Sandell and Sandell 1991, 51), and like in West Greenland they often appear in pairs (Fig. 3.6). The pairwise occurrence of twisters leads to the conclusion that the East Greenland cable backing was arranged in two twisted bundles (comp. Fig. 2.7).

Unfortunately, not many arrow fragments from East Greenland are known (Map 2), but the few that can be studied are characterised by very sturdy dimensions of around 1.5 cm shaft diameter, a round or oval cross section at mid-shaft and a flattened, flared proximal end the width of which exceeding 2.0 cm (Larsen 1934, 70; fig. 22,2.3; pl. 4,3; Ryder 1895, 308; Thomsen 1917, 409; pl. XVIII,7.8) (Pl. 29; Appendix A7–10). Two decayed arrow shafts excavated together with a bow in Jameson Land originally measured more than 50 cm in length (KNK 566 – Tuborg Sandell and Sandell 1991, 55) as also two grave finds from Clavering Island mentioned by Larsen (1934, 70) and a stray find from Snenæs mentioned by Thomsen (1917, 409). According to Ryder (1895, 303), there is

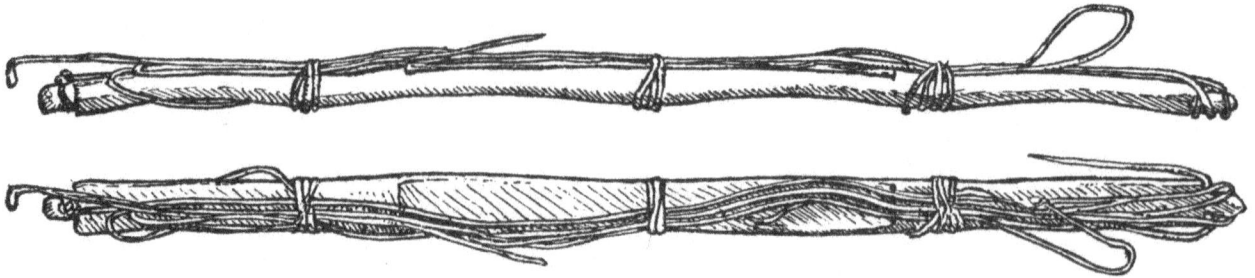

Fig. 3.5 Bow model from Northeast Greenland. Length 16.5 cm (Richter 1934, fig. 2.53).

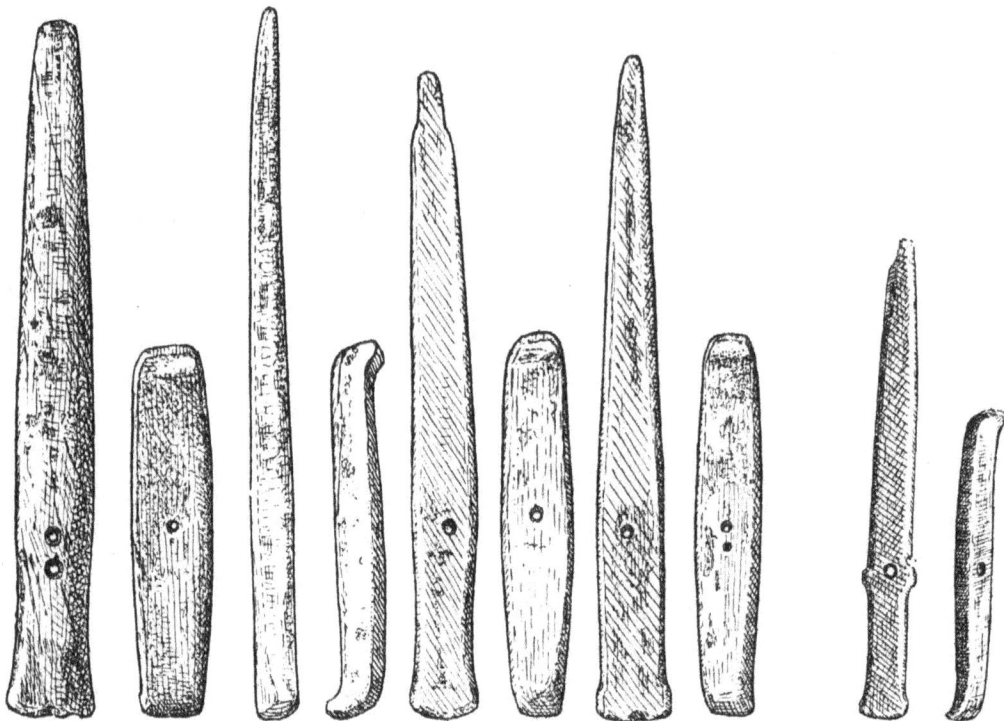

Fig. 3.6 Cable twisters and marlin spikes from Northeast Greenland. No scale (Richter 1934, fig. 2.55).

some evidence of spliced arrow shafts. The fletching is tangential and rather short (Larsen 1934, pl. 8,17) (Pl. 29: L 1.6657). The great majority of arrow points from Northeast Greenland are made of caribou antler. The blades are typically lanceolate and have a biconvex or triangular cross section. Uni- or bilateral barbs are only very rarely found. The tang is conical and has a short, interrupted thread (Mathiassen 1929, 151; Richter 1934, fig. 2.54; Ryder 1895, fig. 3.2; Tuborg Sandell and Sandell 1991, 51). In some cases, it is wedge-shaped (Larsen 1934, pl. 12,2) (Fig. 3.7). Only one single specimen from Dødemandsbugten site, attributed by Larsen (1934, pl. 12,6) to the second phase of his 'East Greenland Mixed Culture', shows a long continuous screw thread. Point lengths range from ten all the way up to 30 cm (Larsen 1934, 70; 107; 145; fig. 22,5–7; pl. 4,3; Mathiassen 1929, 146; 151; fig. 1,6.7; Ryder 1895, 304; Thomsen 1917, 408; Tuborg Sandell and Sandell 1991, 51; fig. 24). Osseous foreshafts with slits for small triangular slate points also occasionally occur, but unlike the examples from West

Greenland they are un-barbed (Glob 1935, 78; Larsen 1934, pl. 12,5; Ryder 1895, fig. 3.1; Thomsen 1917, fig. 20; Tuborg Sandell and Sandell 1991, fig. 24,12) (Fig. 3.7: 16–18).

A typical handle made of tusk from a grave at Dødemandsbugten (Larsen 1934, fig. 22,4) shows that the quiver-bow case combination was also used in East Greenland.

3.4. Miniature bows

Table 5 and Plate 30 give examples of Thule bows from various sites in West and East Greenland in the National Museum of Denmark the dimensions of which being well below those of full-size hunting weapons. The staves of these small bows are made from wood and baleen. Most of them sport rather crudely made d-profiles, but some show the same careful workmanship and complex profiles of the big weapons.

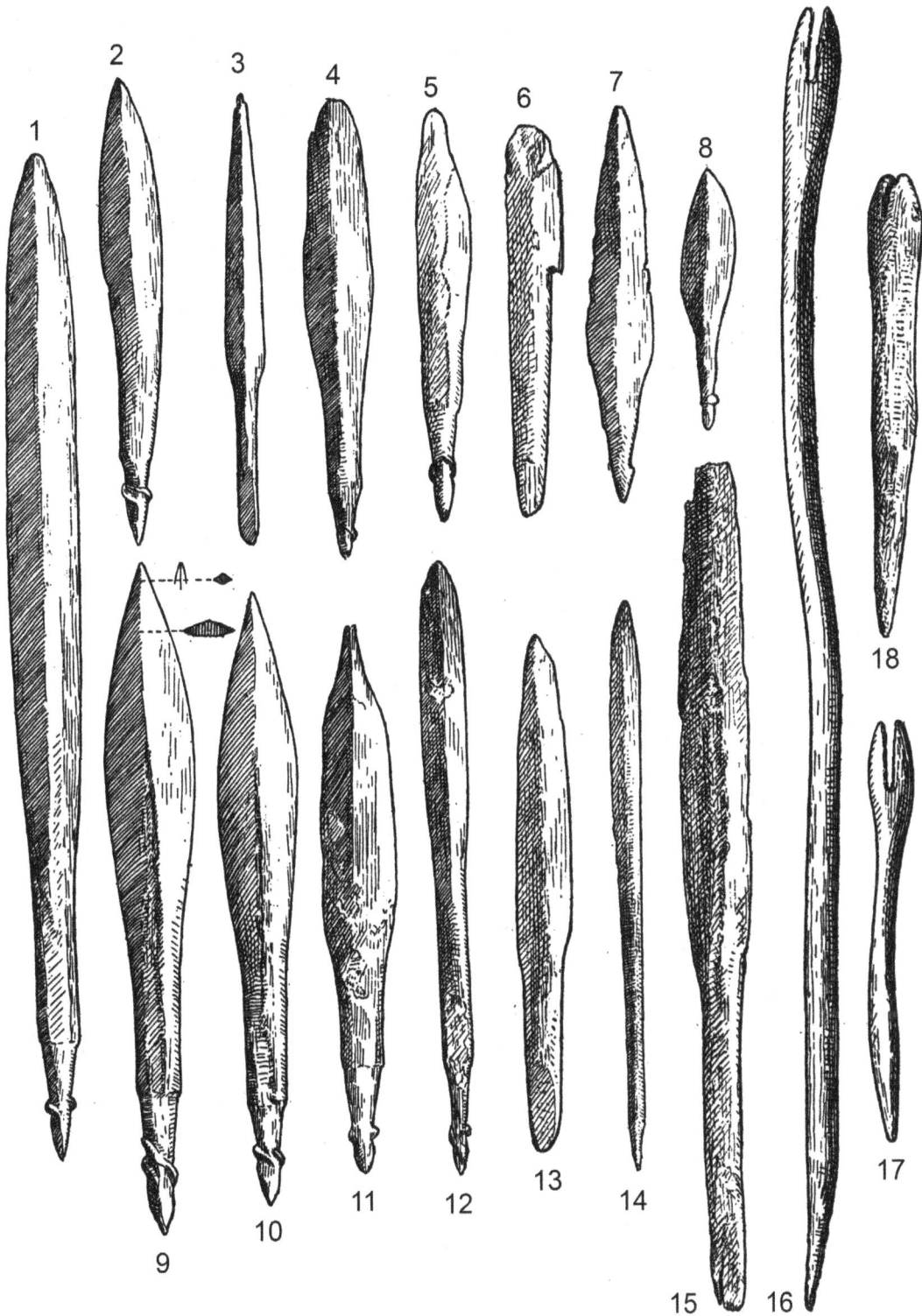

Fig. 3.7 Arrowheads from Northeast Greenland. No scale (Richter 1934, fig. 2.54).

Miniature baleen bows with total lengths ranging from 36–46 cm have also been found in substantial numbers in early Thule contexts in Polar Greenland (Hardenberg 2009, 58; tab. 5,10.11; Holtved 1944, 211), Central West Greenland (Gulløv 1997, 213 ff.; 312 ff.;) and at Dødemandsbugten site in Northeast Greenland (Larsen 1934, 105). Miniature versions of all kinds of tools and utensils are ubiquitous at Thule sites in Greenland (Hardenberg 2009) as well

as other Arctic regions (Kenyon and Arnold 1985; Mathiassen 1927a and b; McCullough 1989). How can that phenomenon be explained? First, a general distinction between mechanically functional scaled-down versions of tools and non-functional miniatures has to be made (Hardenberg 2009, 71). In the case of small bows, the examples given in Tab. 5 and Pl. 30 can be deemed functional, whereas the small model on Fig. 3.5 would not

Tab. 5 Studied miniature bows of the Greenland Thule culture

Inv.-number	Provenance	Total bow length (cm)	Profile	Raw material
L 6.964	Central West Greenland (Illutalik)	no inf.	no inf.	baleen
L 8.2530	Central West Greenland (Sermermiut)	no inf.	no inf.	baleen
L 8.1027	Central West Greenland (Sermermiut)	no inf.	no inf.	baleen
L 8.2531	Central West Greenland (Sermermiut)	no inf.	no inf.	wood
L 8.2545	Central West Greenland (Sermermiut)	no inf.	no inf.	wood
L 8.3286	Central West Greenland (Sermermiut)	no inf.	no inf.	wood
L 12.1674	Central West Greenland (Qeqertarmiut)	76 (reconstructed)	triple curved	wood
L 12.2019	Central West Greenland (Qeqertarmiut)	60 (reconstructed)	recurved	baleen
L. 2245	West Greenland	50 (reconstructed)	d-bow	wood
L 3.11837	West Greenland	53.5	d-bow	baleen
L 3.11838	West Greenland	39.1	d-bow	baleen
L. 3414	Northeast Greenland (Renskæret)	50 (reconstructed)	d-bow	baleen
L. 3439	Northeast Greenland (Renskæret)	60 (reconstructed)	recurved	baleen
L. 3440	Northeast Greenland (Renskæret)	50 (reconstructed)	d-bow	baleen
L 1.3591	Northeast Greenland (Geographical Society Ø)	60 (reconstructed)	d-bow	wood
L 1.5909	Northeast Greenland (Gefionshavn)	no inf.	d-bow	wood
L. 3244	Northeast Greenland (17 Kilometernæsset)	100 (reconstructed)	triple curved	wood
L. 3662	Northeast Greenland (Stormbugtens Østkyst)	100 (reconstructed)	d-bow	Wood

shoot arrows. Non-functional miniatures may have served as pastimes, spiritual objects/amulets, grave offerings, or for illustrative purposes (comp. Gulløv 1997, 213; Hardenberg 2009, 57; 72). Functional miniature bows according to ethnographic observations within Inuit societies at the beginning of the 20th century were used as child's toys being strictly connected to the male sphere (Balikci 1989; Birket-Smith 1945; Jenness 1922; Hardenberg 2009). Consistent with this, in 18th century West Greenland, Hans Egede (1741, 324) observed that boys as soon as they could walk were given miniature weapons by their male relatives and encouraged to constantly practise with them. In societies whose survival depended to a large degree on the expert handling of manifold hunting weapons, it was essential to get accustomed to them as soon as possible – in the case of archery to develop both physical strength and accuracy as well as to learn relevant hunting strategies (comp. Bohr 2000, 10 ff.). Hardenberg (2009) convincingly applies the theory of Situated Learning developed by Lave and Wenger (1991) to the Greenland Thule culture, "with children using miniature replicas of adult tools to gain skills in preparation for future tasks. Thus, toys used in Thule culture played a dual role by providing both an entertainment for children as well as serving as a platform for socialization" (Hardenberg 2009, 82). Against that background it becomes clear that with the small bows from Greenland the transition from toy to tool was a gradual one. As the child grew up, its bow grew with it, evolving from a plaything (e.g. Tab. 5 and Pl. 30: L 1.3591) to a teenager's bow (e.g. Fig. 3.3) and finally to a full-weight hunting weapon (e.g. Fig. 3.2).

3.5. Chronology

Concerning chronology, it has to be pointed out from the beginning that none of the studied bows and arrows is directly dated. Thus, all information on the development of Greenland Thule archery equipment must be elicited from its context. In the case of stray finds, this is hardly possible. Though many of the early archaeological excavations have seen a revision, the scientific methods applied back then limit the informational value of the find materials to some extent (Gulløv 1997, 434 ff.) The ethnographic objects are much better documented and can, moreover, be confronted with the contemporary ethno-historical record. Yet, these observations can be inconsistent as well.

3.5.1. Earliest and latest Thule archery in Polar Greenland

The earliest Thule culture settlements in Greenland date to the 13th–14th centuries (Gulløv 2016, 900). The archaeological sites of Uummannaq and Nuulliit in the Thule region as well as the name-giving Ruin Ø off the cost of Inglefield Land are connected to the pioneering Ruin Island phase (Holtved 1944; Gulløv 2005, 292 ff.; McCullough 1989), whereas the contemporary sites of Cape Kent and Inuarfissuaq in Inglefield Land seem to belong to a different tradition with strong Late Dorset influences (Appelt and Gulløv 1999, 65; Bandi 1965, 134; Gulløv 2005, 295 ff.) Extensive archery equipment was found at all these sites (Holtved 1944, 211 ff.; 1954, 66 f.), and also on the other side of Smith Sound on Ellesmere Island (Alix 2009, 152; fig. 2; McCullough 1989, 113; pl. 13). The method of assembling the wooden bow stave from several pieces by means of v-scarfs was widely applied (Holtved 1944, pl. 10,17–19; McCullough 1989, 113; pl. 13). Baleen bows appear in substantial numbers in early Thule context, most of them probably made for children (Holtved 1954, 66). However, there are also short but very sturdy laminated weapons of that type with cable backings (Holtved 1944, 211; pl. 47,6–8; McCullough 1989, 111; pl. 12e–h). Some antler bows are reported as well (Holtved 1944, 211; pl. 10,20), but it cannot be excluded that these are more recent, intrusive elements, the emergence of which relates to a phase when wood and baleen became increasingly scarce in Polar Greenland (Mathiassen 1927, 44). Flat or d-shaped bracers were used to support the joints (Holtved 1944, 212; pl. 10,21–23; McCullough 1989, pl. 14h–m). As far as can be judged, the profile of the early Thule bows is either recurved or pronounced triple-curved (Holtved 1944, pl. 47,8; Maxwell 1985, 274; McCullough 1989, pl. 12d–h). The backing is always the single-cable Eastern type and made of sinew or baleen (Holtved 1944, 211; McCullough 1989, pl. 12d.h). The arrows of the earliest Thule culture are generally short with flattened, widened nocks and a tangential fletching. Their distal ends have closed sockets. In many cases, the wooden shafts are spliced (Holtved 1944, 215; McCullough 1989, 122; pl. 12a–c; 16) (Fig. 3.8: 6–10). The tusk and antler arrow points of the Ruin Island facies are lanceolate or triangular, often with uni- or bilateral barbs bearing inscribed lines, and have tangs with either a ring-like collar or a bulb (Holtved 1944, 214; pl. 11,23.29; pl. 12,1; McCullough 1989, 120; pl. 15) (Fig. 3.8: 1 and 2). Foreshafts with slits or blade beds occasionally occur (Holtved 1944, pl. 11,23.24; McCullough 1989, pl. 15d.k). The same types are encountered in Central Arctic Canada dating perhaps to the 12th and 13th centuries (Mathiassen 1927a, 154; pl. 8,2–7; McGhee 1984, 373), and in Western Thule context where they date to ca. 1000–1400 AD (Giddings and Anderson 1986, 70; 74; pl. 15; 31; Mason and Bowers 2009, Fig. 2.4). Still further west, in the Bering Sea region, the design can even be traced back to the preceding Punuk culture (Bandi 1995, Fig. 2.6).

In addition, there are numerous arrowheads with staggered knob tangs (Holtved 1944, pl. 11) (Fig. 3.8: 3 and 4), a type which is also frequently encountered in house ruins attributed to the Late Dorset culture (Gulløv 2005, 287; 292). Outside Greenland, it seems to be rare as, for example, from the big Central Arctic sites of Naujan and Qilalukan only a few specimens are reported (Mathiassen 1927a, pl. 9,4.6; 42,10). It seems that two different contemporary arrowhead designs existed in Polar Greenland: one with clear Early Western Thule roots, and one with a more eastern 'imprint' that possibly emerged due to some Late Dorset influences – with the caveat that to date there are no bow or arrow finds that can be attributed to these last Greenlandic Palaeo-Inuit (Appelt 2005, 197). Quiver handles of antler and tusk, sometimes richly ornamented, are very common in the earliest Greenland Thule culture both in Thule and Inglefield Land (Gulløv 2005, 306; Holtved 1944, 214) (Fig. 3.8: 12–21).

Based on these observations it can be concluded that all the characteristic features of Arctic archery equipment were fully developed when the Thule culture reached Greenland.

During the 17th century, the Thule region was heavily depopulated as a consequence of the Little Ice Age (Gulløv 2005, 339), and the bow was not in use when in the early 1860s a group of Inuit immigrated from North Baffin Island (Birket-Smith 1918, 8). Their spliced Central Arctic antler composite bows and arrows with split or scarfed distal ends (Boas 1907, fig. 189; Mathiassen 1927b, 44; 1945, 55; fig. 24; 200) were immediately adopted by the remaining Thule population and employed for caribou hunting until the late 1890s when the gun had finally replaced them (Birket-Smith 1918, 8; Malaurie 1990, 184). Unlike in the early Thule culture (Alix 2009, 151), wood and baleen were not used in these late bows because both resources were not abundant anymore in Polar Greenland (Mathiassen 1927b, 44). In Peary Land, the Thule culture was present only during a short period of time in the 15th century (Grønnow and Jensen 2003, 211). The famous Kolnæs site from ca. 1500 AD (Knuth 1952) yielded a wooden bow tip and several arrow shaft fragments as well as a complete arrow of 31.5 cm length with an ivory head (Grønnow and Jensen 2003, Fig. 2.7,7). Their small dimensions suggest an interpretation as toys.

3.5.2. Parallel traditions in West Greenland

Soon after its arrival to Greenland, the Thule culture quickly spread south reaching Disko Bay and the Sisimiut region during the 14th century (Grønnow et al. 1983, 68; Gulløv 2016, 901). The beginning of the Thule occupation at the big winter settlement of Sermermiut (Gulløv 1997, 441; Mathiassen 1958) possibly relates to that time period. Unfortunately the Thule stratigraphy that stretches all the way up to the 19th century could not be differentiated precisely (Mathiassen 1958, 42). Yet, the lower deposits of the midden yielded numerous miniature bows of wood and baleen (Tab. 5; Pl. 30) closely resembling the contemporary specimens from Polar Greenland. All arrowheads excavated by Mathiassen are of antler and lanceolate with one, two or without barbs and have a conical tang with two staggered knobs (Mathiassen 1958, tab. 3). Additionally, there is a small collection of arrowheads with screw tangs from Sermermiut, but their context is unknown (Pl. 25: L. 1693–1696). The lowest part of the Illutalik midden (Mathiassen 1934) dates to the 15th century (Gulløv 1997, 439 f.) Apart from wood, baleen was also used for bow staves (Mathiassen 1934, 97; pl. 5,1.10). The arrowheads are all of antler and lanceolate with one, two or, prevailingly, without barbs. Mathiassen (1934, 97) notes that in the lower midden there are only knob tangs, whereas in the upper layers screw tangs occur as well. The Inussuk site, dating to the 15th century (Gulløv 1997, 442 f.), matches that observation. Every single specimen of the 57 antler arrowheads recovered has a knob tang (Mathiassen 1930, 195 f.; pl. 7). The

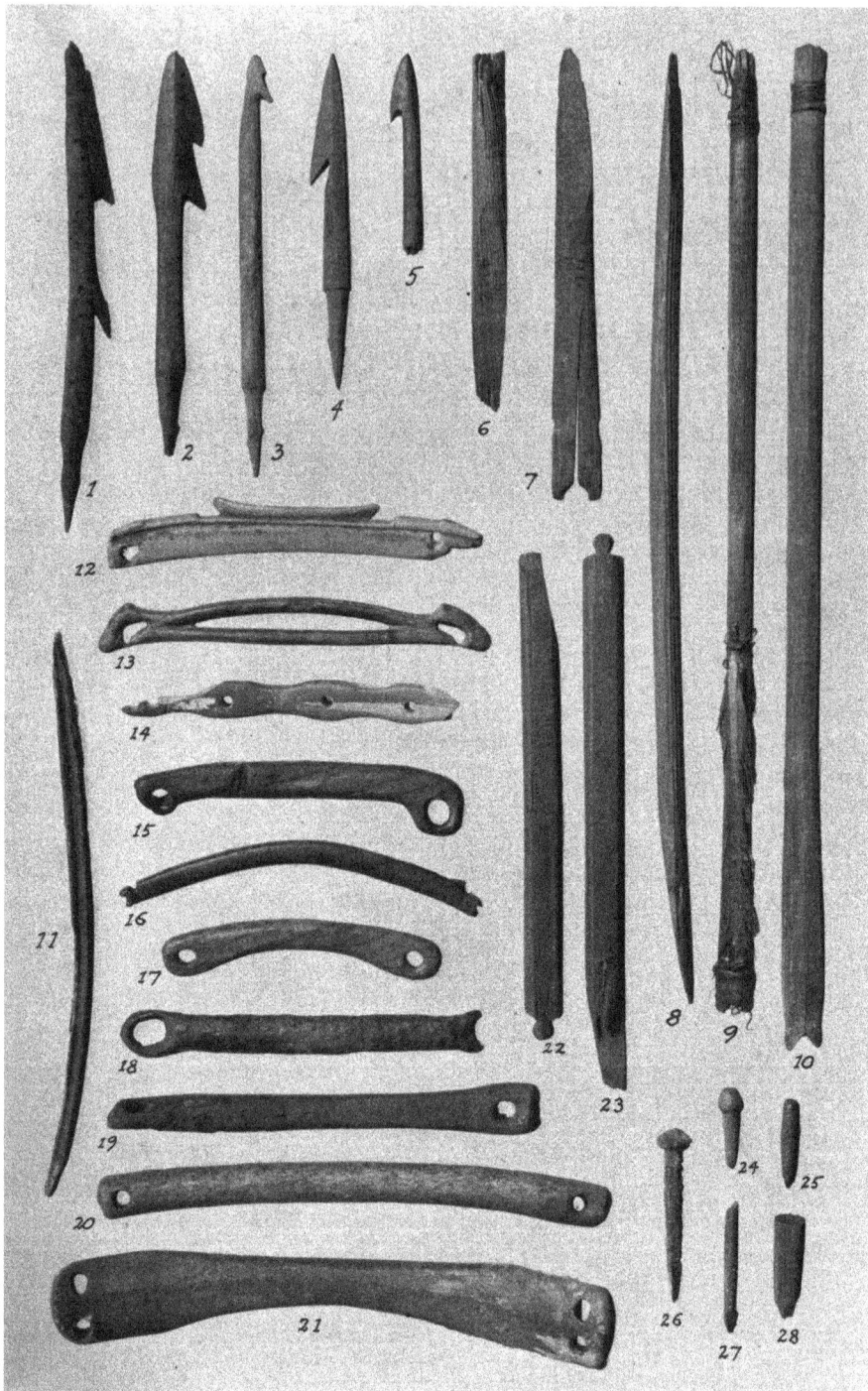

Fig. 3.8 Arrowheads (1–5), shafts (6–10) and quiver handles (12–21) of the earliest Thule culture in Polar Greenland. No Scale (Holtved 1944, pl. 12).

bows are spliced wooden or laminated baleen composites (Mathiassen 1930, 194; pl. 6; 21).

Further south, at Qeqertarmiut site (Mathiassen 1931), the earliest remains of the Thule culture date to the 16th century (Gulløv 1997, 437 f.). Both wooden self bow staves and laminated baleen bows are represented (Mathiassen 1931, 80 f.) One tiny wooden specimen is triple-curved and shows the typical paddle shaped silhouette with contractions at mid-limb (Pl. 30: L 12.1674). The arrowheads are of antler and lanceolate with one, two or

without barbs. Again, there are only knob tangs in the lower midden and screw tangs are restricted to the upper layers (Mathiassen 1931, 81).

In the Nuuk Fjord, the Thule culture is present from the 14th century onwards (Gulløv 1997, 435). The archery equipment from Kangeq and Illorpaat, consisting of wooden bow tips, arrow shaft fragments and antler arrowheads with knob or screw tangs (Gulløv 1997, 138 f.; 300 f.), can mainly be dated to the 16th century (Gulløv 2005, 318 f.) One fragment from Illorpaat has a single longitudinal groove on the back, possibly to receive a single-strand cable backing (Gulløv 1997, 138 f.) If that interpretation is correct, then in the 16th century Nuuk Fjord system the Eastern backing type was used. Some arrow fragments have very unusual split front ends to receive the head (Gulløv 1997, 140). John Davis' contemporary descriptions of Inuit hunting equipment mention the extensive use of bow and arrow in this region (Bugge 1930, 51; Gulløv 1997, 392).

For the 17th century, there are two important ethnographic testimonials of archery equipment: the highly-detailed Bergen painting from 1654 (Pl. 31) and the Kunstkammer bow (Pl. 19: Lb. 1; 21). Both share a wooden stave about 130 cm long, a baleen strip on the back and a twisted cable backing of the Arctic type. However, the painted bow has a d-profile, while the other one is triple-curved. Obviously, two different contemporary bow designs existed side by side in the Nuuk Fjord system. Parallel design traditions are not unusual in the Arctic: Among the Netsilik on King William Land, aside from the prevailing short splinted horn and antler composites also the long, scarfed triple-curved wood bow was known (Taylor 1974, pl. 8; tab. 15) (Pl. 36), and the Copper Inuit on Victoria Island at the beginning of the 20th century used simple wooden self bow staves, spliced triple-curves with Arctic backings and short splinted horn/antler bows with Eastern backings side by side (Jenness 1946, fig. 3.81; 152). The 17th century Kunstkammer arrow Lc. 32b, like the one pictured in the Bergen painting, has a one-piece barbed arrow point made from antler (Appendix A7).

In the first half of the 18th century, 'Greenland's apostle', the Norwegian missionary Hans Egede (1741, 354) describes the bow as a hunting weapon every man possessed:

„Men angaaende deres Bue og Pile, hvormed de skyde Dyrene, da ere de nesten saadanne som andre bruge dem. Buen er en god Mands Favn lang og godt seigt Fyrre-Traee, som paa Norsk kaldes Tenal; og paa det den kand vaere dis stivere, belegge de den bag paa med tyk flettet Seene-Traad, og en god sterk Snoer af Saelhunde-Skind eller flettet Seener sammen lagde, som driver Piilen fort. Det fremmerste af Piilen bestaar enten af Jern eller Been, med et Hag eller flere paa, at den ikke skal falde ud igen, naar den bliver skudt i Dyret. Fugle Piilene ere med 2. eller 3. stumpede been paa Enden, for allene døde Fugelen og ikke skamfere Kiødet.“

"Their bows and arrows which they use to shoot animals are almost similar to those used by others. The bow is about man-high and a well grown piece of pine which in Nordic language is called tenal; and for making it stiffer they use to put thick, plaited sinew tread on the back and a good, strong string of sealskin or plaited sinews that casts the arrow. The foremost part of the arrow consists of either iron or bone, with one or several barbs to prevent it from falling out again when once shot into the animal. Bird arrows have two

or three blunt pieces of bone attached to the ends to just kill the bird without destroying the skin".

The ethnographic bow in Trondheim (NTNU Vitenskapsmuseet 2008, 62), the bow pictured in the Copenhagen painting of the famous West Greenlanders Qiperoq and Pooq from 1724 (Pl. 32), and the weapons in a drawing by H. Egede from the year 1737 showing a fictional fighting scene between Norse and Greenlandic Inuit (Pl. 33) are all d-bows of considerable length. Both great length and simple profile are also reported by Fabricius (1818, 235) in the beginning of the 19th century. Based on this information it can be concluded that the typical bow in 18th century Central West Greenland was a longbow with a d-profile (comp. Thomsen 1928, 320). The complex recurved and triple-curved designs of the early Thule culture had obviously become so unusual at that time that Egede could use them as a characterising feature of the Norse in his above-mentioned drawing. The corresponding arrows are of considerable length and usually have osseous foreshafts with barbs and riveted metal points (Fabricius 1818, 238; NTNU Vitenskapsmuseet 2008, 62; Pasda 2011, 54) (Pl. 25). One studied arrow (Pl. 22 and 24: Lb. 430a) has a triangular front end, probably for fastening three separate osseous pieces. Maybe this is one of the 'bird arrows' mentioned by H. Egede. The bow went quickly out of use in West Greenland during the 18th century in favour of muzzle-loaded firearms (Birket-Smith 1918, 9; Cranz 1770, 194; Glahn 1771, 230). In the years around 1770 according to Fabricius (1818, 235), it already had become a curio from the olden days. Very likely, this is the reason that some of Fabricius' information on the weapons' construction sounds quite odd. First, he mentions separate spliced-in bow tips of osseous material, called innursaursak due to their man-like appearance. Second, he writes that the whole bow stave is 'notched' to prevent the transverse sinew wrappings that hold the cable backing in place from shifting (Fabricius 1818, 236 f.). Though both features are well-known in Arctic bow making traditions elsewhere (Birket-Smith 1945, fig. 18; Boas 1901, Fig. 3.15; 86; 1907, fig. 189), they are not found at all in the extensive material record from West Greenland. Thus it is likely that these technological details provided by Fabricius are not based on his personal observations but rather on some possibly unreliable memories of Inuit informants. The very cursory illustrations (Fabricius 1818, fig. 1–3) further support this notion. For Disko Bay, Porsild (1915a, 159 f.; fig. 20) also refers to notched bow staves. However, two specimens he collected there (Pl. 10: L. 4568 and L. 4569) are not notched, and he also admits that his descriptions are largely based on 'memories and scarce notes' (1915a, 159).

As a consequence of the hostilities between Denmark and Great Britain during the Napoleonic Wars in the first decade of the 19th century causing a severe shortage of both gunpowder and ammunition, a return of the bow and arrow for caribou hunting in West Greenland is postulated (Grønnow 2009, 201; Pasda 2011, 54; Secher et al. 1987,

68). A few Inuit informants refer to that distant time in the beginning of the 20th century (Grønnow et al. 1983, 27; Petersen 2003, 141). However, the scale of that short renaissance that – if at all – happened when the West Greenland caribou population was anyway quite low (Meldgaard 1986, fig. 3.8; 16), is difficult to judge: There is no conclusive evidence of bow and arrow in the material record from that time (e.g. at the big summer camp of Aasivissuit – comp. Grønnow et al. 1983, fig. 2.70; 72), and it is also difficult to imagine how the complex archery technology could have been revived after it was widely abandoned more than one generation before. The famous water colours with caribou hunting scenes by Aron of Kangeq (born 1822) from the middle of the 19th century (Meldgaard 1982, 24 f.) frequently picture stylised 'classic antique' bows and even simple back quivers (Pl. 34) that are not documented anywhere else in Greenland. Therefore it is very likely that – contrary to Hans Egede a century before him – this otherwise highly accurate Inuit artist had not seen the West Greenland hunting bow in practical use again.

Concerning the grave, surface and stray finds from West Greenland which represent the great majority of the studied material admittedly their chronological position within the Thule culture remains very rough (Appendix A1 and 2). In principle, any dating from the 15th to the 18th century is conceivable. The laminated baleen bows from Northwest Greenland may be quite ancient as this bow type already shows up in the earliest archaeological sites and the big baleen whales became very scarce from the 17th century onwards (Birket-Smith 1918, 23). Arrowheads with screw tangs according to the archaeological evidence emerged not earlier than during the 16th century, whereas the knob tang appears to run through all time periods. Both the triple-curved bow and the one-piece antler arrow point seem to be rather archaic elements that had gradually fallen into disuse by the end of the 17th century. On the other hand, the long d-bows and arrows with barbed antler foreshafts and metal points from Central West Greenland are probably the youngest phenomena and would date to the late 17th to late 18th century and hence the early colonial period.

3.5.3. Continuity in East Greenland

By 1400 AD, immigrating groups originating from the Thule region had settled most parts of coastal Northeast Greenland, finally reaching Scoresby Sound by 1500 AD at the latest (Gulløv 2005, 282; Sørensen and Gulløv 2012, 94 f.). Then again, in summer 1823 on a beach on Clavering Island the Englishman Cpt. Douglas Charles Clavering incidentally encountered a small group of Inuit most likely belonging to the very last Thule inhabitants of Northeast Greenland (Gulløv 2009). The numerous archery finds from that vast region thus should date sometime between 1400 and 1800 AD, but a finer chronological differentiation within these four centuries is hardly possible (Glob 1946, 38; Grønnow and Jensen 2003, 340; Gulløv 2005, 308 ff.). The occupation of the big Dødemandsbugten site (Map 1) starts in the 15th century (Gulløv 2005, 310). Based

on house architecture and artefact types, Larsen (1934) distinguished two phases within his 'East Greenland Mixed Culture'. However, in both stages arrowhead tangs with a short interrupted screw thread are typical (Larsen 1934, 107; 145). The grave No. 6 at Dødemandsbugten with bow and arrows as well as an ivory quiver handle (Larsen 1934, fig. 22) likely dates to the 15th or 16th century (Gulløv 2005, 306). All antler arrowheads have interrupted screw tangs. The excavated structures in Jameson Land (Map 1) might be as young as the beginning of the 19th century (Gulløv 2005, 313; Tuborg Sandell and Sandell 1991, 93). Again, all arrowheads have interrupted screw tangs. Occasionally, and likely contemporaneous with the interrupted screw tang, arrowheads with wedge-shaped tangs are attested in Northeast Greenland (Glob 1937, pl. 5,11; Richter 1934, fig. 2.54, 13) (Fig. 3.7d). Throughout the 16th to 18th centuries excursions were made by Northeast Greenlanders to the Ammassalik region in Southeast Greenland, which was permanently settled during the 17th century (Gulløv 2005, 311; Sørensen and Gulløv 2012, 99). This provides a time frame for the few bow finds from there (Map 1). As the Ammassalik caribou probably already died out between 1200 and 1500 AD (Meldgaard 1986, 43), the archery equipment from this region should not be of local origin but rather relate to the recurrent migrations from the Northeast.

Both archery design and technology in East Greenland are markedly uniform and continue the early Thule traditions from Polar Greenland to the very end. Concerning the bows, this is represented by the ancient triple-curved profile and the reconstructed Eastern cable backing type. The extensive use of baleen in the early phases (Larsen 1934, pl. 9) is another archaic element. The short interrupted screw tang of the arrowheads might well have derived from the old staggered knob tang common in Thule and Inglefield Land. The progressing geographical isolation of the East Greenland Thule population from the second half of the 15th century onwards in relation to the Little Ice Age (Sørensen and Gulløv 2012, 100) probably fostered the emergence of two marked regional idiosyncrasies. The first is the formal decline of the triple-curved bow design. While the very pronounced bends and sharp angles characteristic of the early Thule culture bows were retained in West Greenland (Pl. 11), the East Greenland triple curved specimens are most often so slightly bent that they appear almost straight (Pl. 26). Thus, they can be interpreted as design rudiments reflecting an ancient tradition but not being mechanically functional anymore. Second, the technique of heat bending wooden bow staves to shape was abandoned and the shallow curves in the East Greenland bows were invariably carved out from the full material.

3.5.4. Arctic backing and screw tang – two Greenlandic innovations?

Based on this chronological overview, two conspicuous phenomena of Greenland archery may be briefly discussed. As has been shown, the bows of the early

Thule culture had cable backings of the one-layer Eastern type which already Murdoch (1890, 308) and Birket-Smith (1918, 25) considered to be the most ancient one. However, eventually in West Greenland the two-layer Arctic backing resting on shoulders came into being. Birket-Smith (1918, 25), Boas (1901, 64) and Mathiassen (1927b, 43) all localise the origin of the Arctic backing tradition in the Thule homeland in the western Arctic, i.e. eastern Siberia and northern Alaska, from where it spread eastward. Regardless of the similarly open question of its emergence there, a diffusion of the concept into Greenland is of course conceivable. Yet, it is equally possible that the Arctic backing was an independent development in West Greenland. The carved shoulders which are distinctively West Greenlandic and do not occur anywhere else in the Arctic would support that hypothesis.

The second question concerns the emergence of the screw tang. Archaeological evidence suggests that it is younger than the staggered knob tang (see 3.5.2.). In West Greenland, it cannot be found prior to the 16th century (Gulløv 1997, 349), but it was definitely already in use before the European whaling period began. Mathiassen (1931, 81) and Maxwell (1985, 276) trace the innovation back to interactions between Thule people and Norse settlers. However, as the Greenland Norse population had vanished already by the early 15th century (Arneborg 2005, 278), a face-to-face transfer of knowledge is unlikely and it is also not supported by the archaeogenetic evidence (Raghavan et al. 2014). The frequent collecting of artefacts in abandoned Norse settlements would be another possibility (Gulløv 1997, 249; 2016). But what screw-like artefacts come into question? Norse arrowheads did not have screw tangs (Arneborg 2005, 270), and neither was the screw used in construction. The only imaginable Norse screw-like tool type would be the spiral drill. Yet, in Greenland there is to date no archaeological evidence of it. Porsild (1915a, 162; 1915b, 15) hence attributes the invention of the screw tang to the West Greenland Inuit themselves, as does Gulløv (1997, 349). This notion is supported by the arrowheads from Northeast Greenland on which a short interrupted screw tang was used, which probably was an indigenous innovation as the region was largely isolated from the 16th century onwards and according to current knowledge had no exposure to the Norse whatsoever.

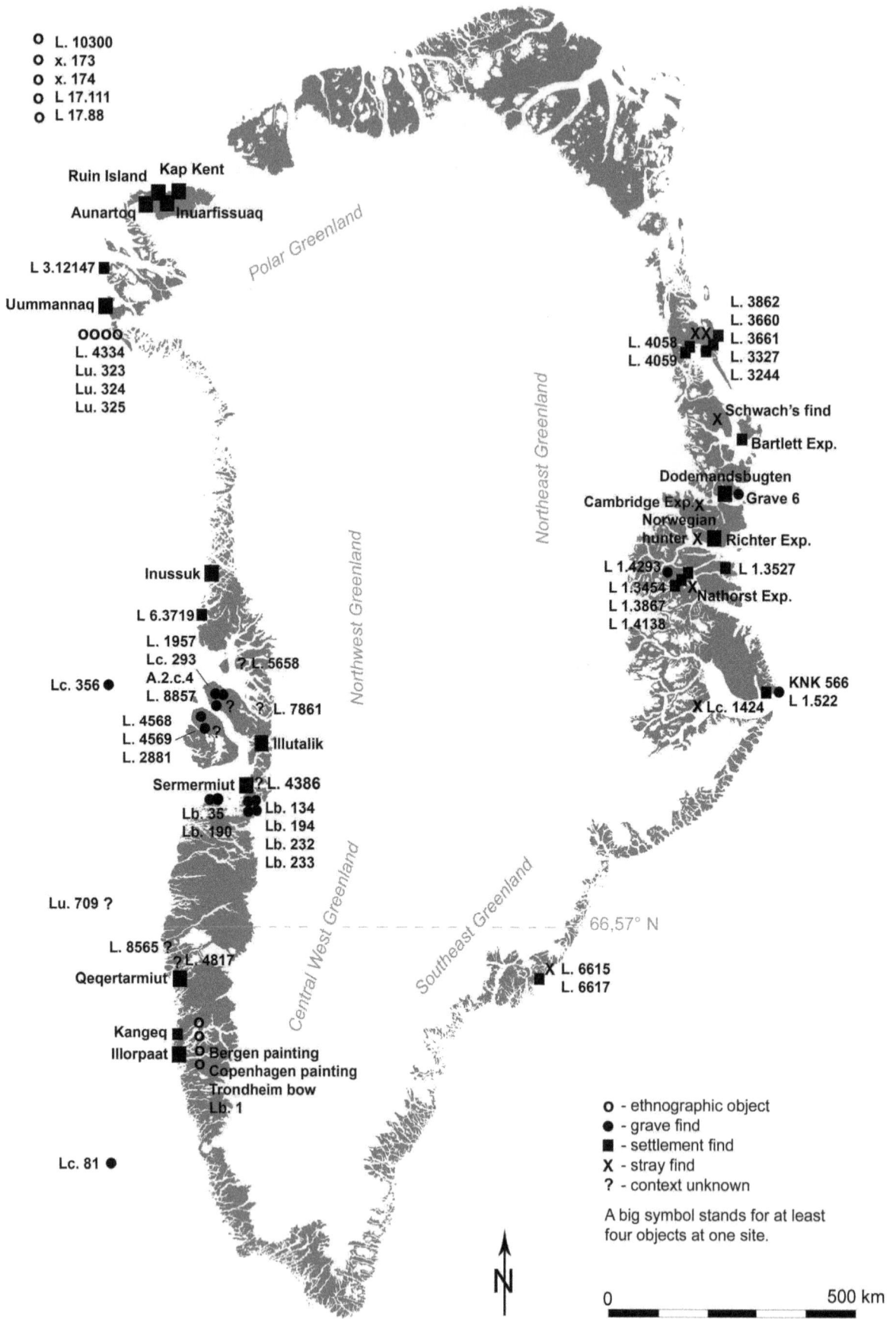

Map 1. Regional distribution of bows of the Greenland Thule culture.

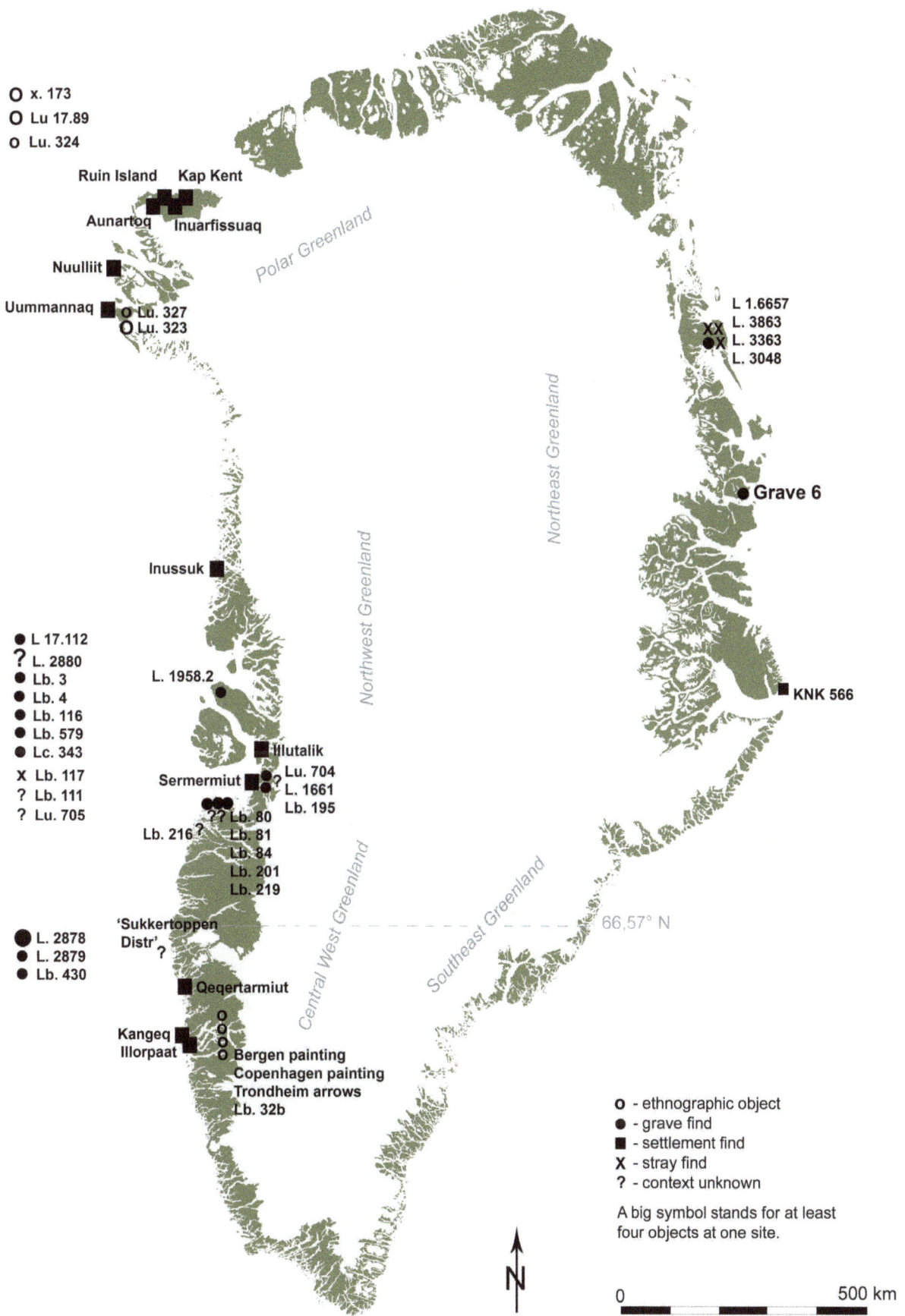

O x. 173
O Lu 17.89
o Lu. 324

Ruin Island   Kap Kent
Aunartoq   Inuarfissuaq
Nuulliit
Uummannaq   o Lu. 327
              O Lu. 323

Polar Greenland

L 1.6657
L. 3863
XX
● X L. 3363
L. 3048

Northeast Greenland

● Grave 6

Inussuk

Northwest Greenland

● L 17.112
? L. 2880
● Lb. 3
● Lb. 4
● Lb. 116
● Lb. 579
● Lc. 343
X Lb. 117
? Lb. 111
? Lu. 705

L. 1958.2

KNK 566

Ilutalik
Sermermiut   Lu. 704
              ● ? L. 1661
              ●●● Lb. 195
              ?? Lb. 80
Lb. 216 ?   Lb. 81
              Lb. 84
              Lb. 201
              Lb. 219

'Sukkertoppen
Distr' ?

Central West Greenland   66,57° N

Southeast Greenland

● L. 2878
● L. 2879
● Lb. 430

■ Qeqertarmiut

Kangeq   o
Illorpaat o
         o
         o Bergen painting
           Copenhagen painting
           Trondheim arrows
           Lb. 32b

o - ethnographic object
● - grave find
■ - settlement find
X - stray find
? - context unknown

A big symbol stands for at least
four objects at one site.

N

0   500 km

Map 2. Regional distribution of arrows of the Greenland Thule culture.

Map 4. Regional distribution of bow technologies.

● - self bow
X - spliced composite bow
■ - laminated composite bow

A big symbol stands for at least four objects at one site.

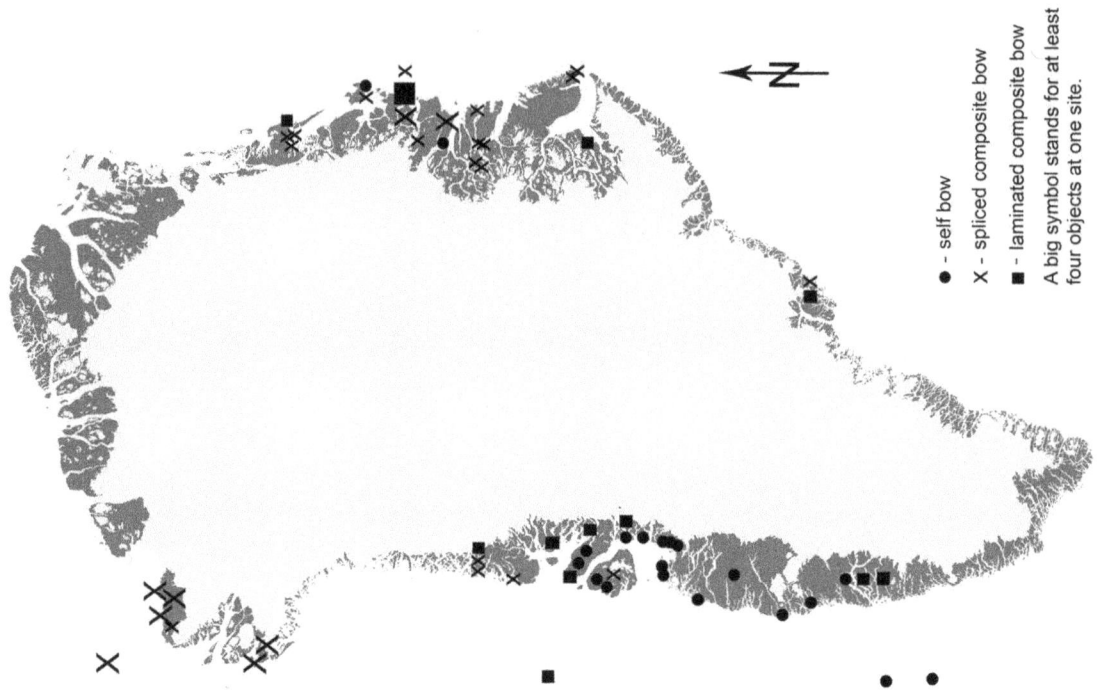

Map 3. Regional distribution of bow raw materials.

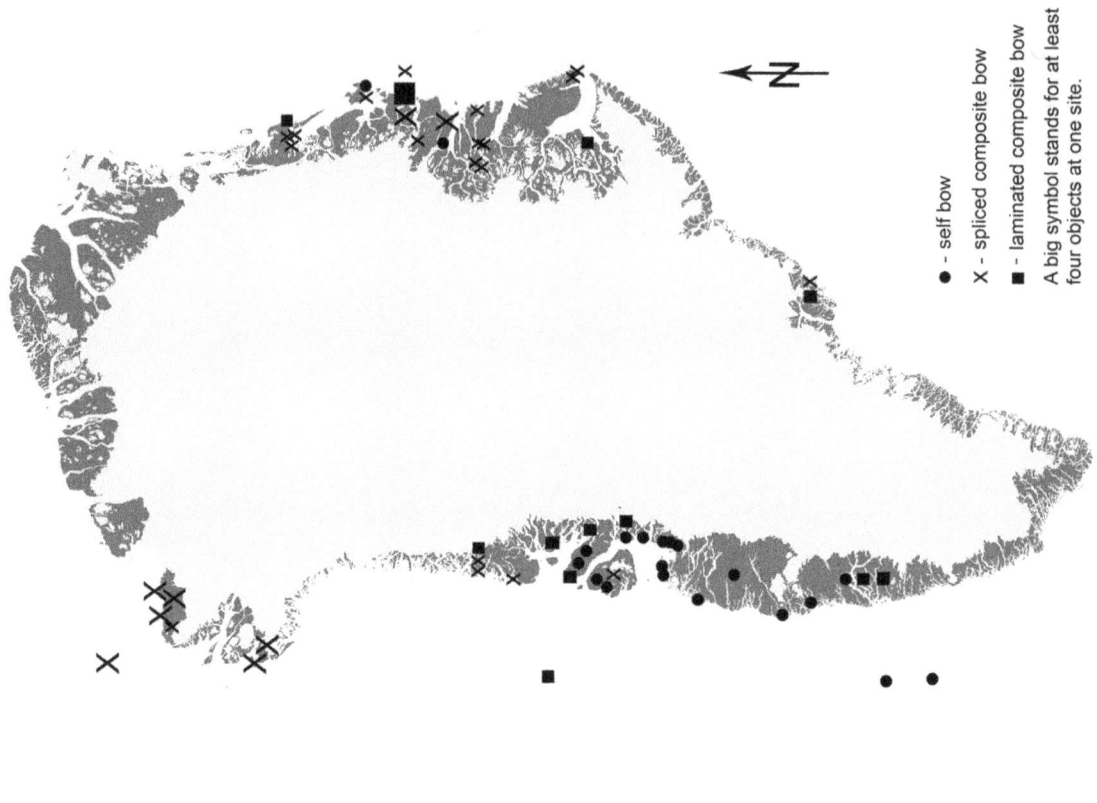

● - wood
X - antler
■ - baleen
O - wood and baleen

A big symbol stands for at least four objects at one site.

Map 6. Regional distribution of bow profiles.

X - double-curved
• - d-profile
O - triple-curved
■ - recurved

A big symbol stands for at least four objects at one site.

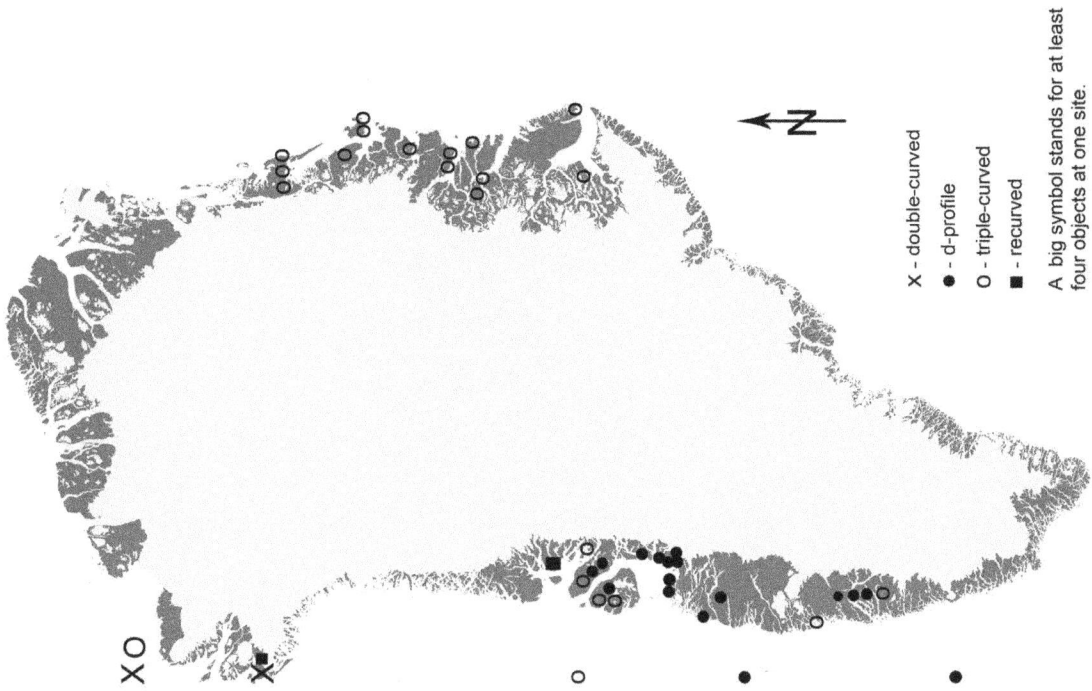

Map 5. Regional distribution of bow limb cross sections

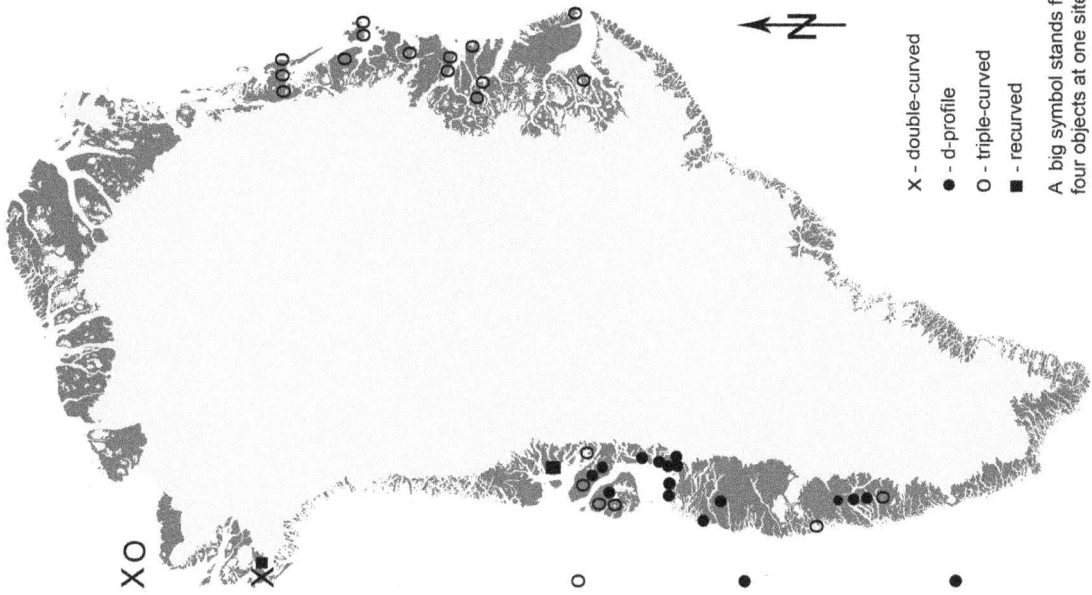

• - d-shaped
O - rectangular
■ - triangular

A big symbol stands for at least four objects at one site.

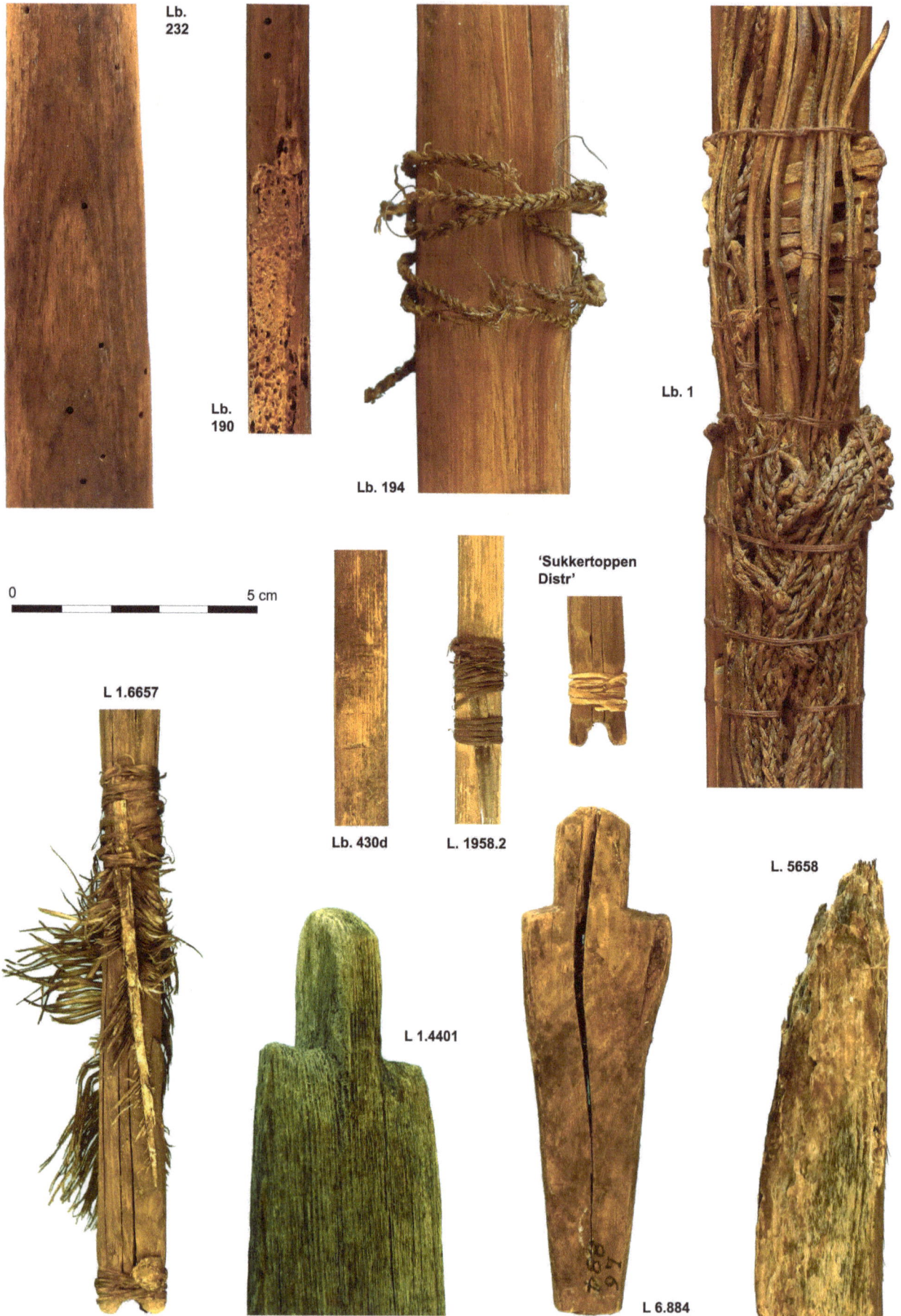

Plate 1. States of preservation.

Lb. 194

Back

Lb. 190

Back

Lb. 35

Side

L. 2881

Belly

0   5 cm

Back

Belly

Back

Lc. 81

Lb. 232

Lb. 1

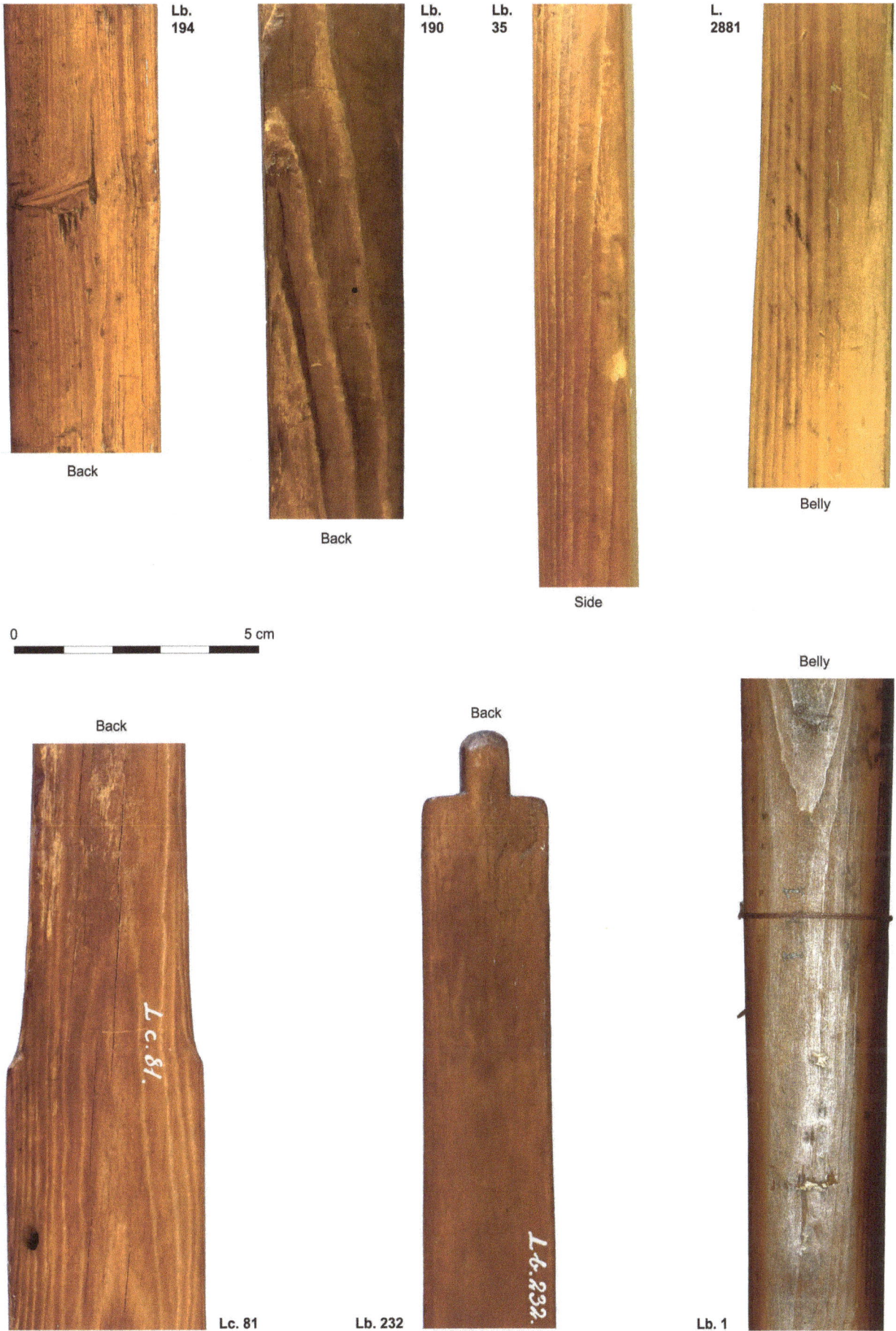

Plate 2. Grain and growth ring orientation.

L 1.4293

Lc. 1424

Lc. 356

Lu. 324

Lb. 1

Lb. 579

0   5 cm

L 17.88

L. 1958.2

Lu. 327b

Lu. 704

Lu. 323d

Lu. 327b

Plate 3. Joints and splices.

x. 174

L. 10300

Lu. 324

L. 17.111

0   20 cm

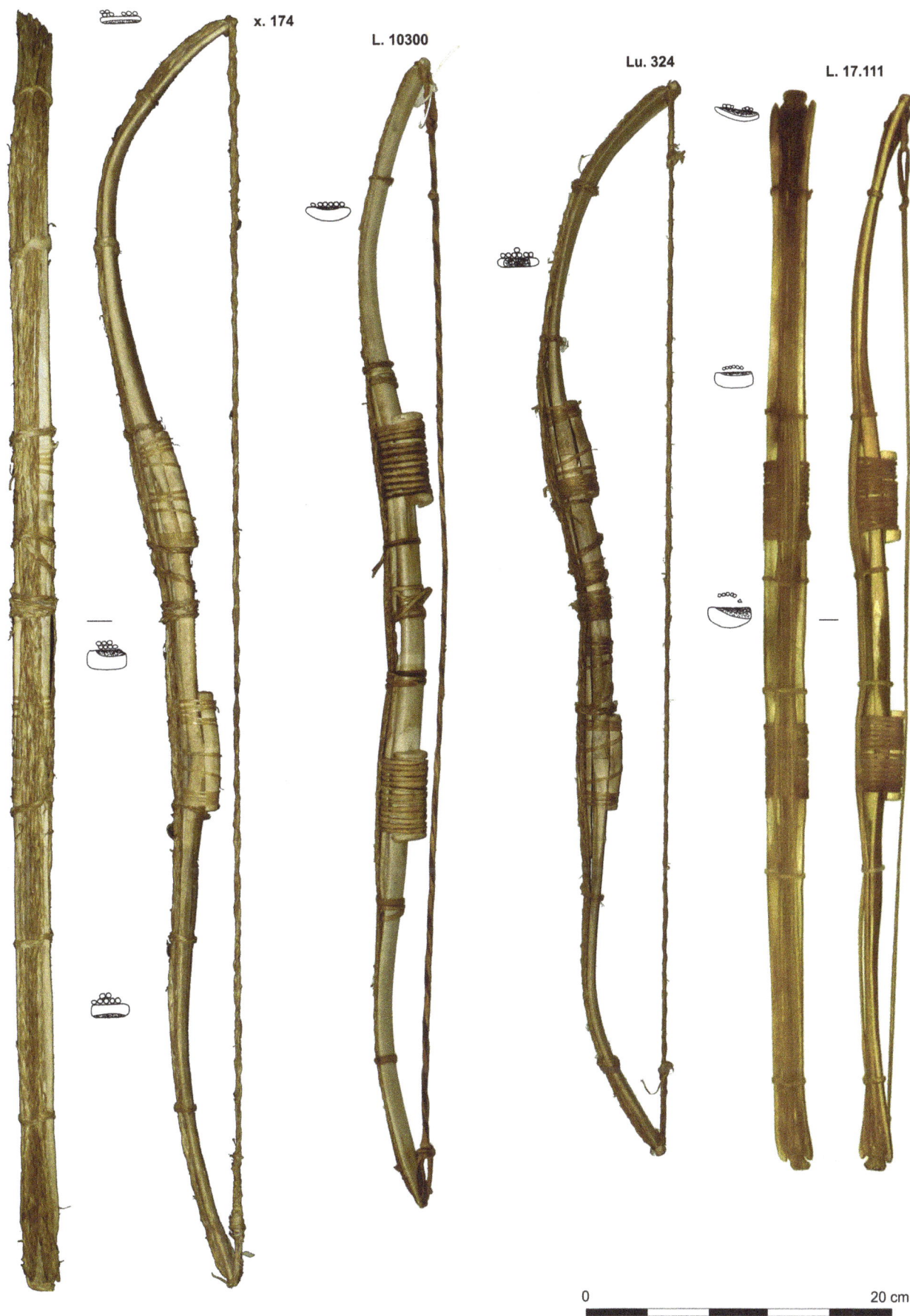

Plate 4. Bows from Polar Greenland.

Lower mid-limb - side

Upper rear end - belly

Lu. 323

Upper mid-limb - side

Lower rear end - belly

Lu. 324

5 cm

5 cm

Upper mid-limb - side

Upper rear end - belly

x. 174

Upper mid-limb - back

L. 10300

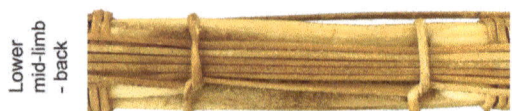

Lower mid-limb - back

Lower mid-limb - side

L 17.111

Plate 5. Bows from Polar Greenland – details.

Lu. 327a

Lu. 705a

Lu. 324a

Lu. 327b

x. 173f

Lu. 323b

Joint

Joint

0   5 cm

0   10 cm

Lu.
324a

Lu.
324b

x.
173c

x.
173d

x.
173g

x. 173g

x. 173d

Lu. 323d

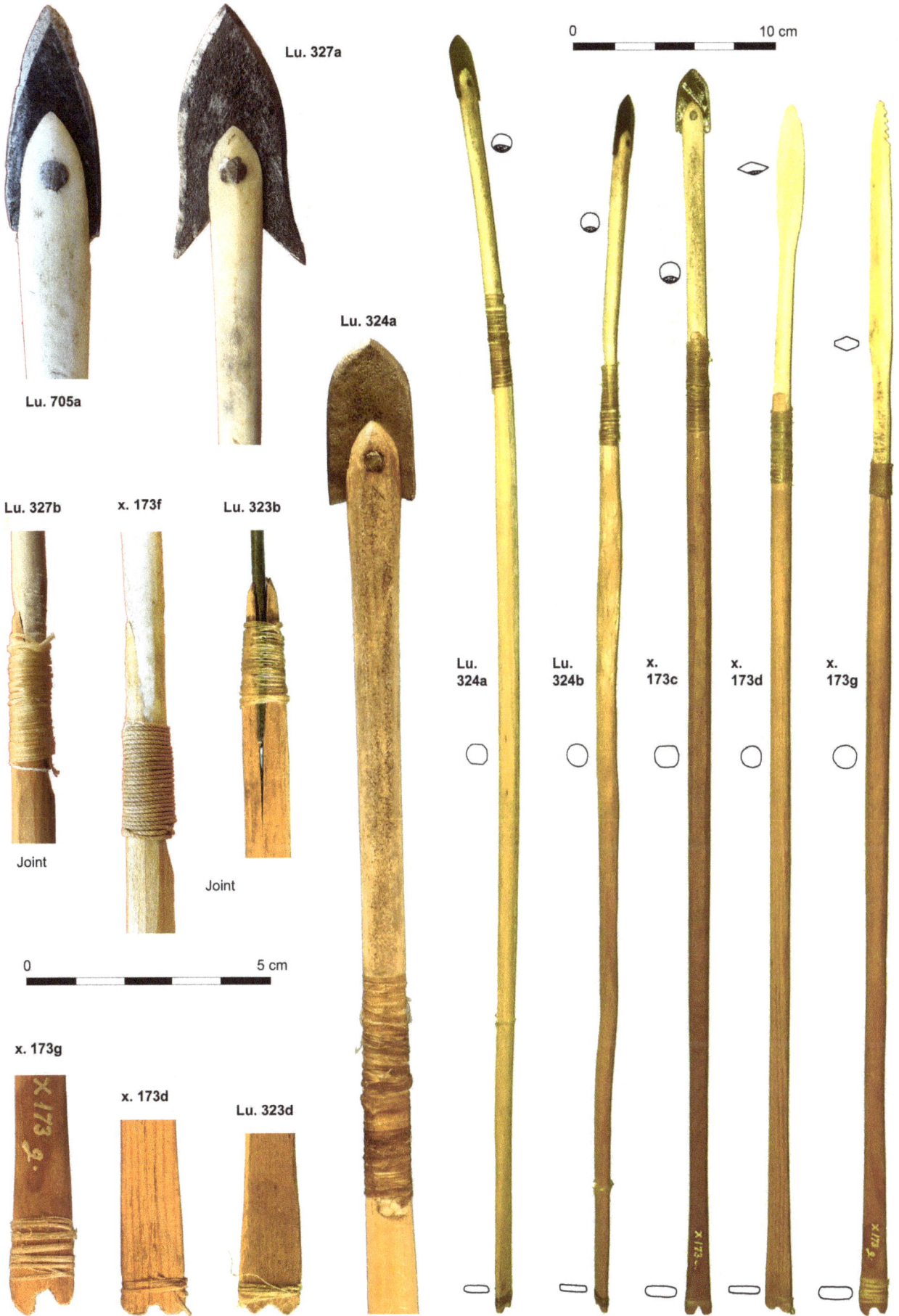

Plate 6. Arrows from Polar Greenland.

Lu. 323

0   20 cm

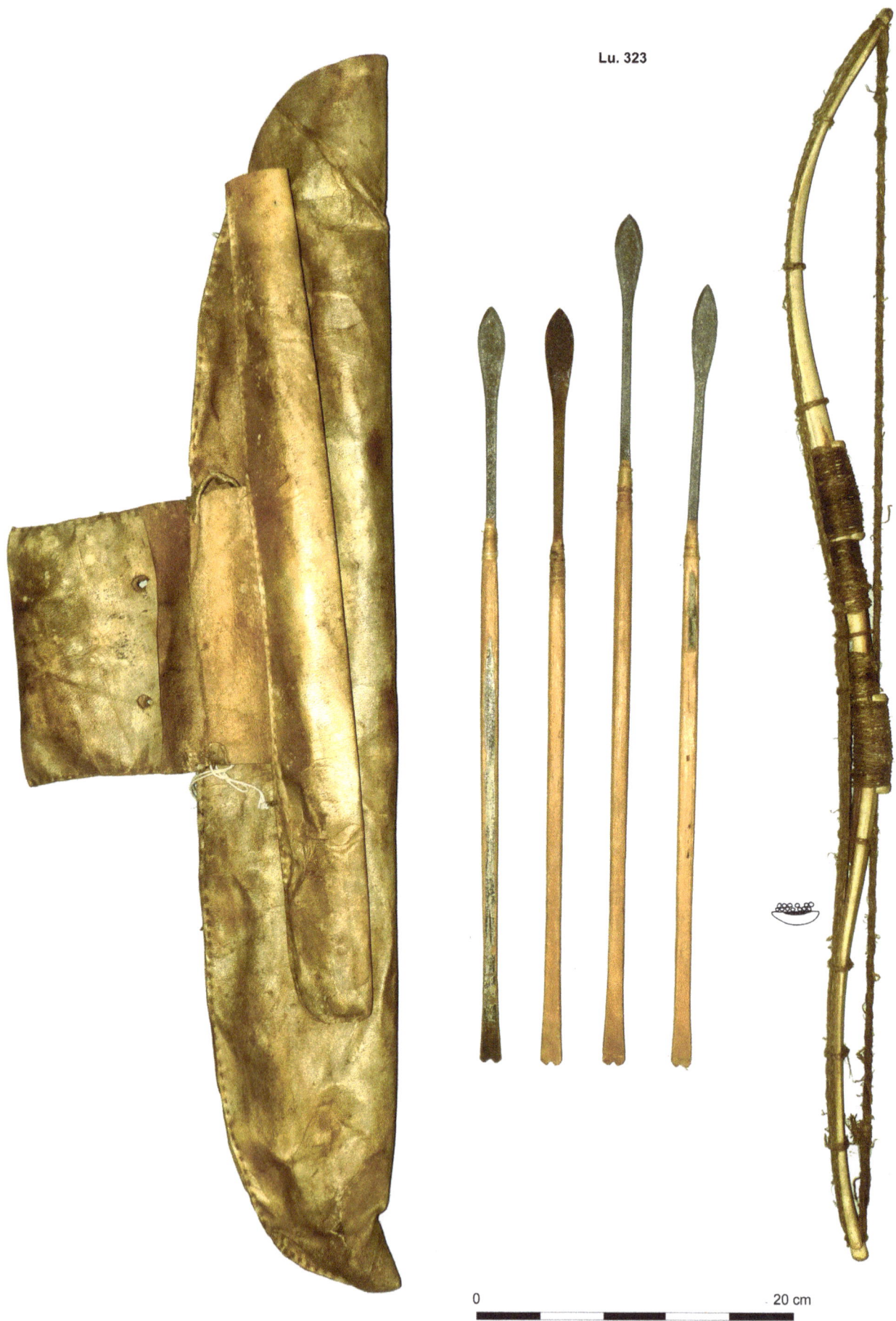

Plate 7. Archery set from Polar Greenland.

Lu. 326

0   10 cm

Plate 8. Miniature archery set from Polar Greenland.

Upper tip
- back

0   5 cm

Upper
mid-limb
- side

L 17.88

0

10
cm

L 17.
89q

L 17.
89o

L 17.
89d

L 17.
89m

L 17.
89a

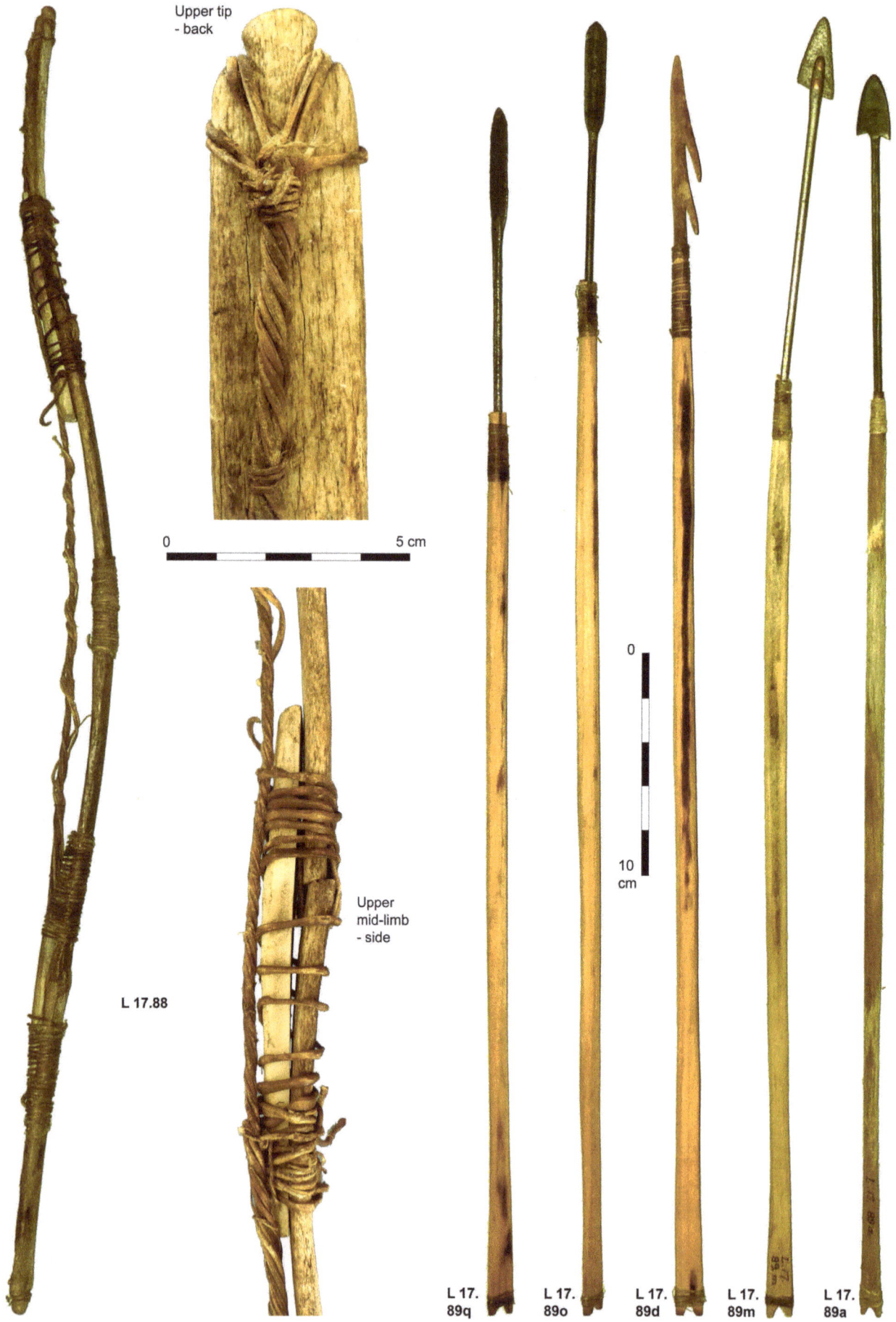

Plate 9. Bow and arrows from Ellesmere Island.

L. 4568

L. 2881

L. 4569

L. 5658

0   20 cm

Plate 10. Bows from Northwest Greenland.

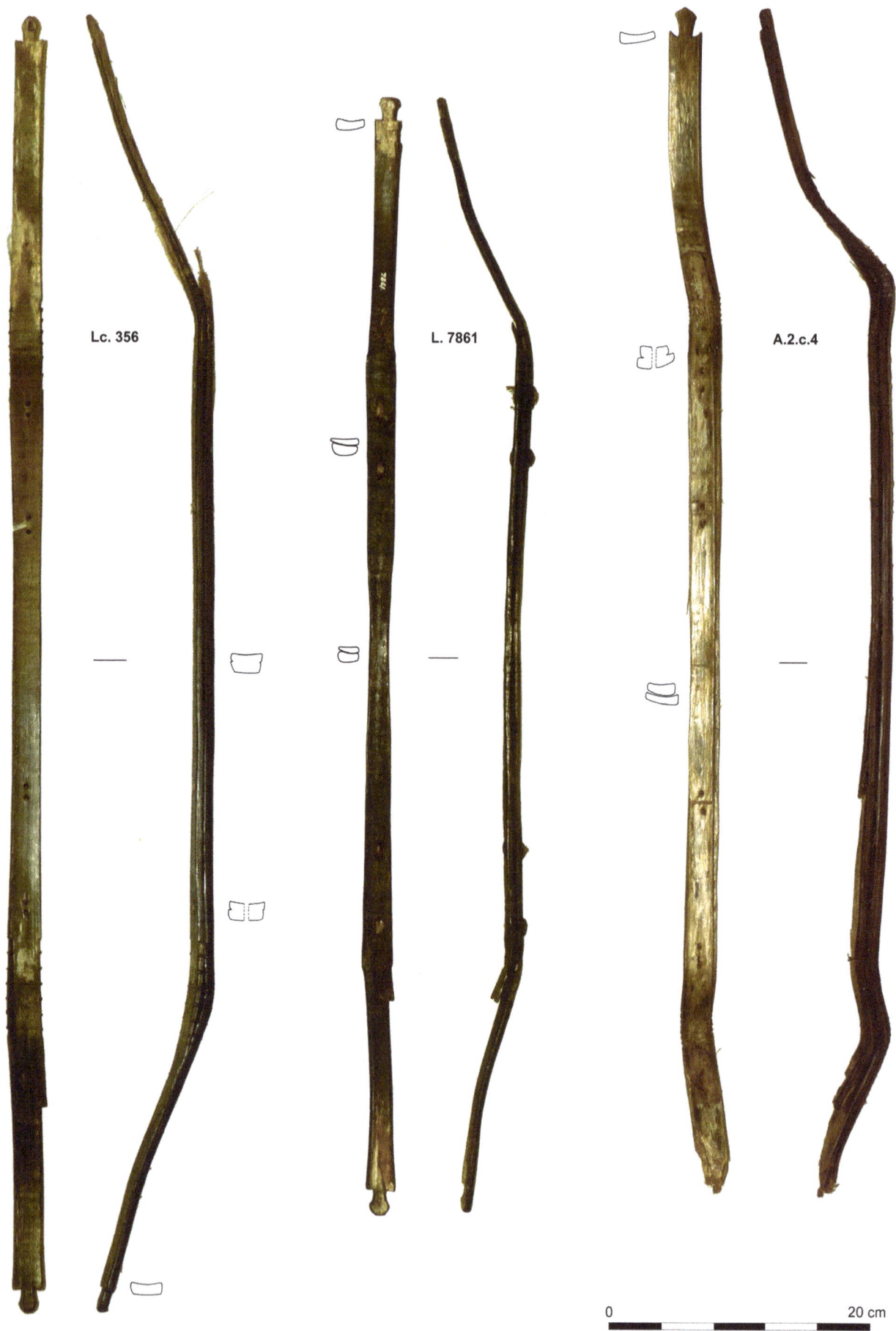

Lc. 356

L. 7861

A.2.c.4

0   20 cm

Plate 11. Baleen bows from Northwest Greenland.

0   5 cm

Upper
mid-limb
- back

Lower
mid-limb
- side

L 6.685

L. 2881

Upper
mid-limb
- side

Handle
- side

L. 4568

Lower tip
- back

L. 4569

Lower tip
- back

Lower
mid-limb
- side

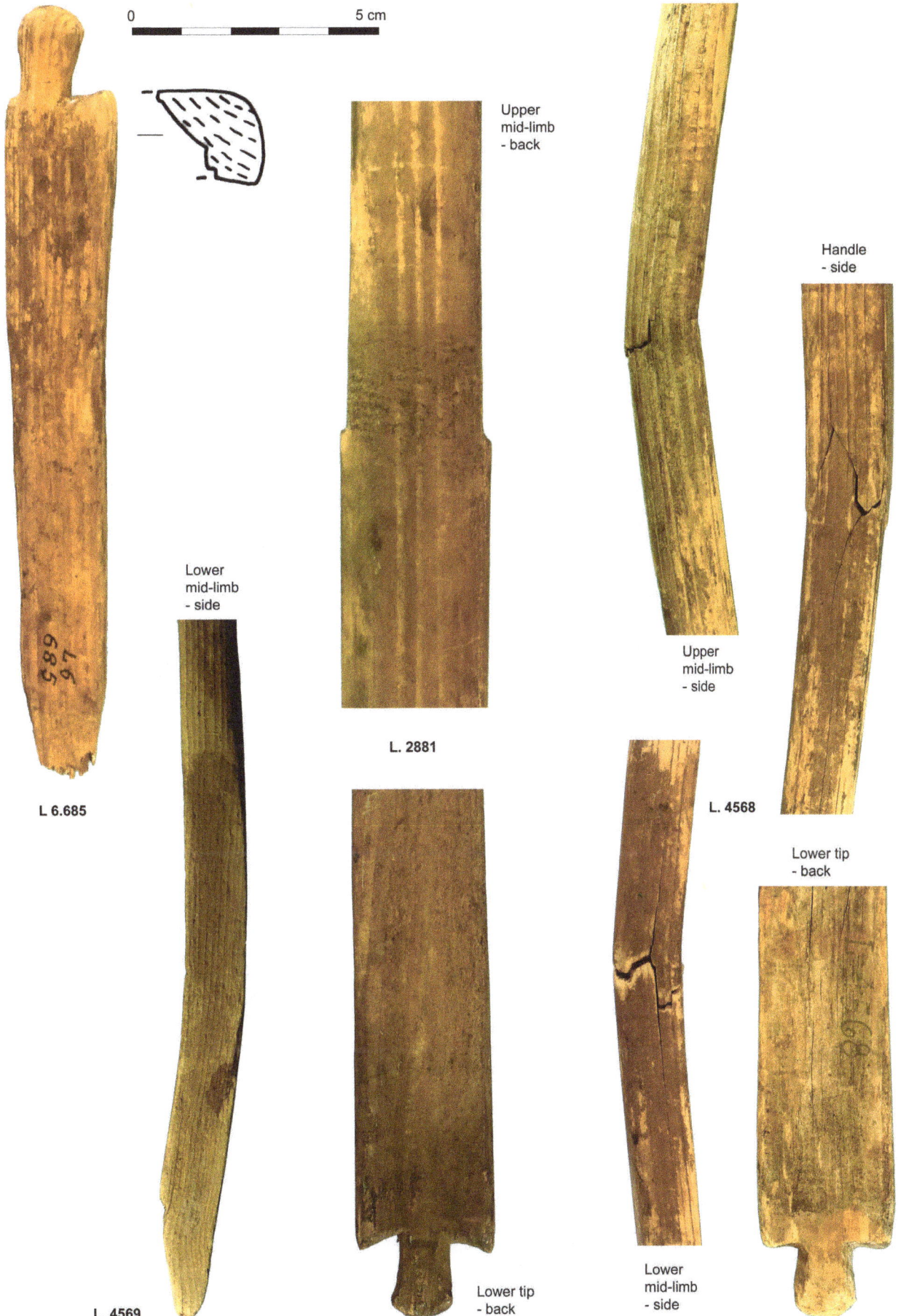

Plate 12. Bows from Northwest Greenland – details.

L 6.781

L. 3327

5 cm

0

Lc. 356

Lami-
nations

L. 7861

Lami-
nations

Mid-
limb
- back

5 cm

0

L. 5658

Mid-
limb
- back

A.2.c.4

Mid-
limb
- back

Mid-
limb
- side

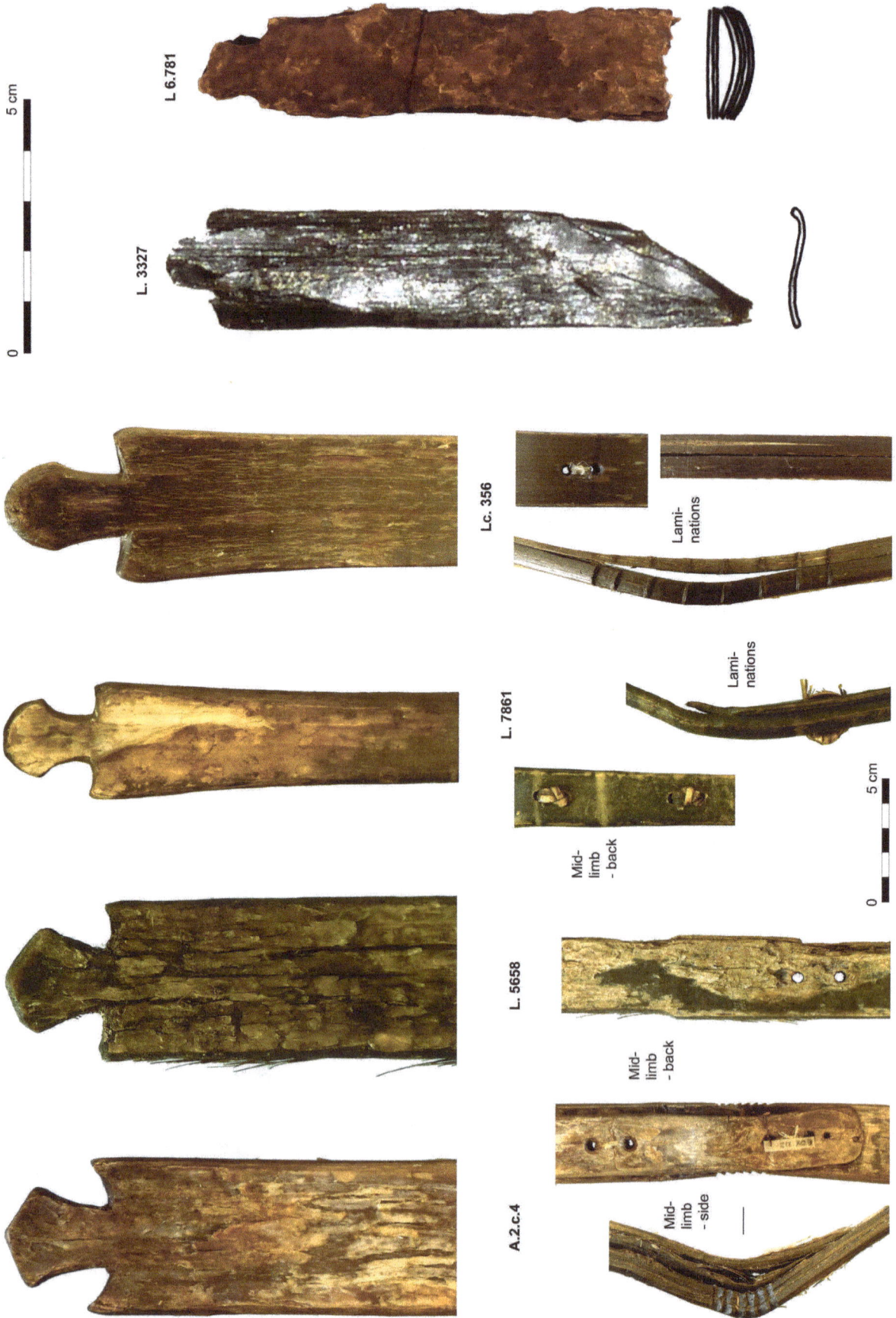

Plate 13. Baleen bows from Northwest Greenland – details.

Lb. 579

L. 1958.2

Lb. 116.1

Lb. 116.2

0   10 cm

Lb. 84

Lb. 111a

Lb. 111b

Lb. 111c

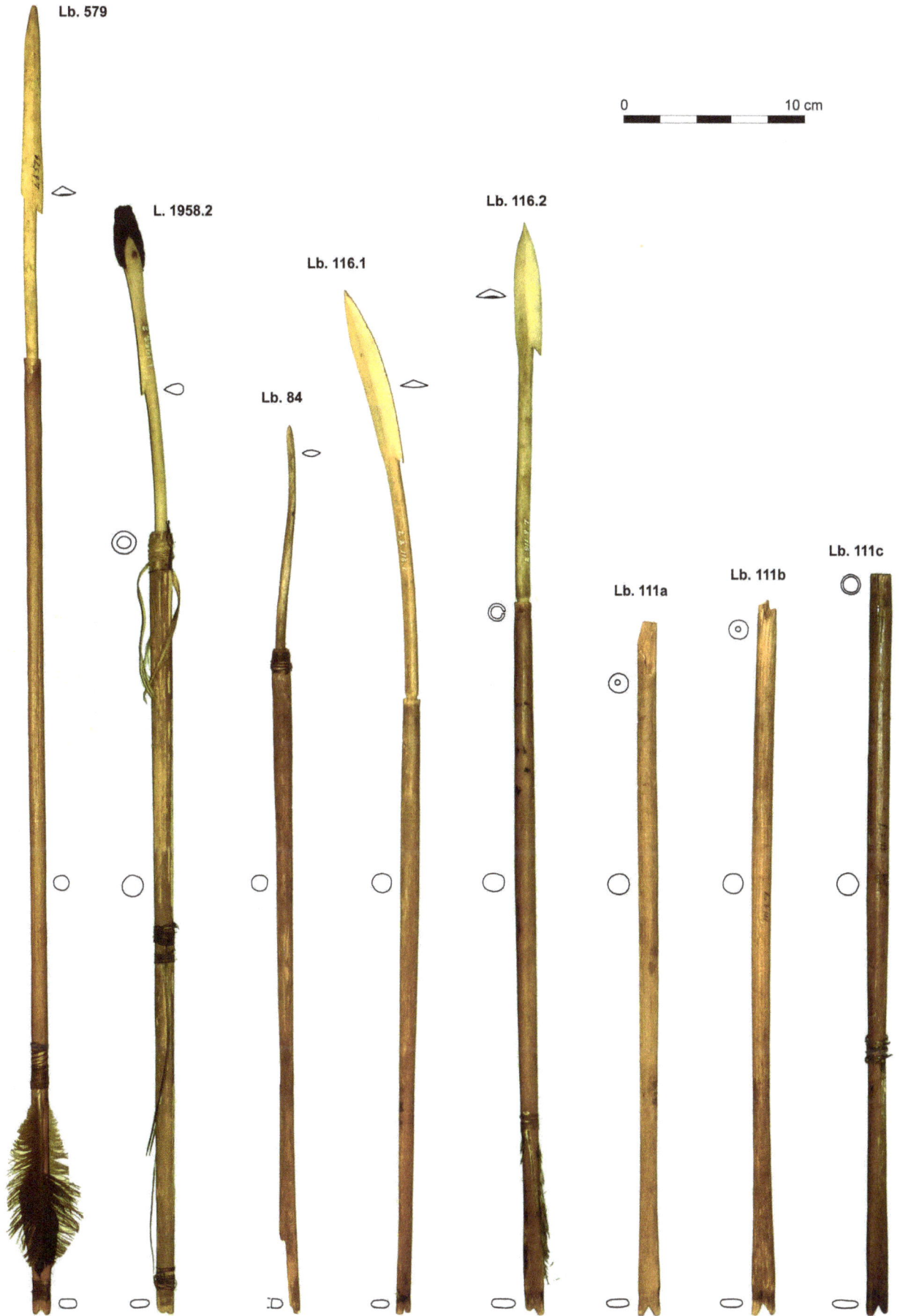

Plate 14. Arrows from Northwest and West Greenland.

0   20 cm

L. 2880d

L. 2880b

L. 2880a

L. 2880c

L. 2880e

Lb. 3

'Sukkertoppen Distr'

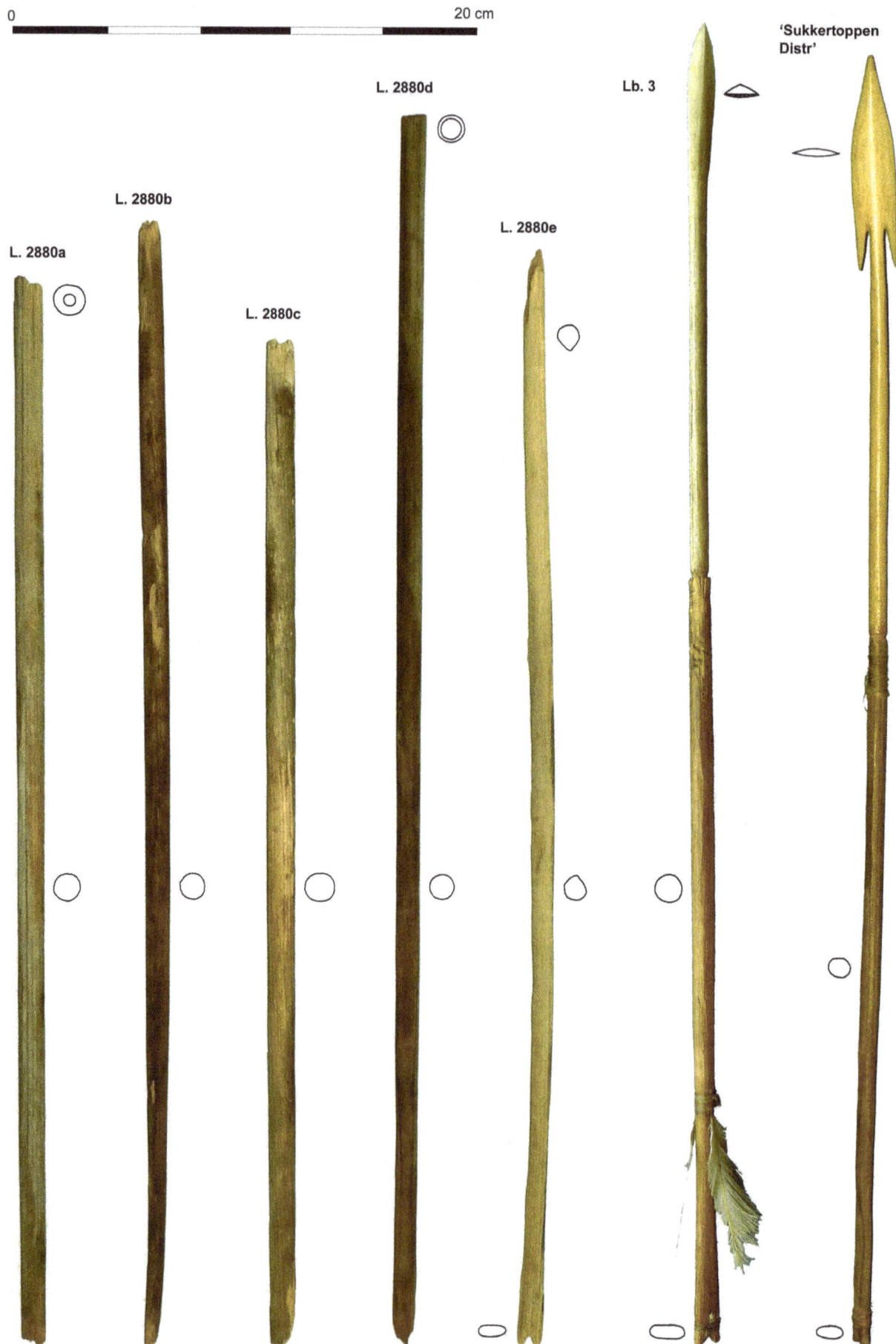

Plate 15. Arrows from Northwest and West Greenland.

Joint

Lb. 3

Wrapping

Lb. 111c

Distal
end

Distal
end

Lb. 111a

Wrapping

Distal
end

Lb. 111b

Nock

L. 1958.2

Joint

5 cm

0

Lb. 84

L. 2.84

Lb. 579

Wrapping

L. 2880e

"Sukkertoppen
Distr"

Joint

Lb. 116.1

Joint

Lb. 116.2

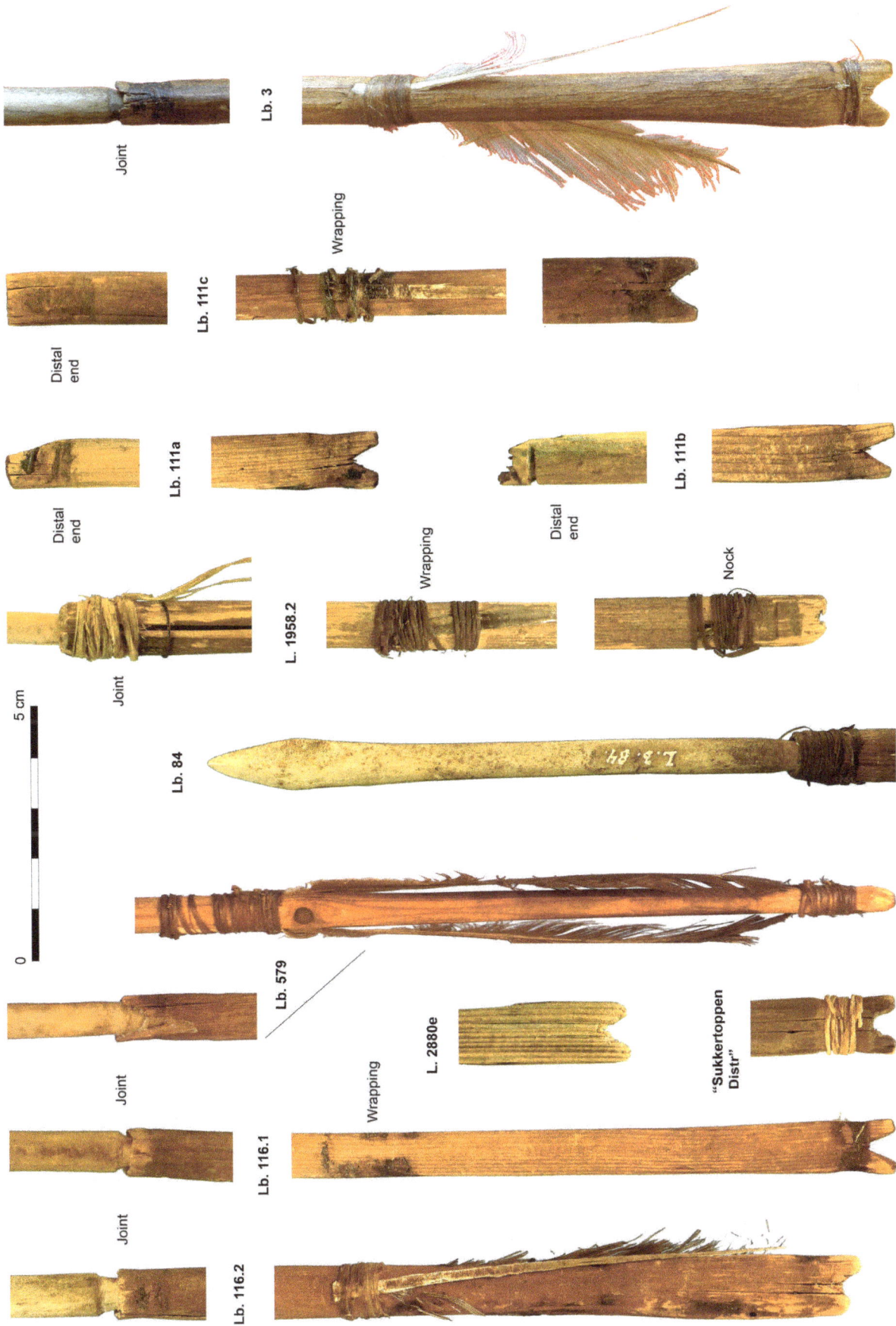

Plate 16. Arrows from Northwest and West Greenland – details.

49

L. 2818
L. 2819
L. 2831
L. 2825
L. 2834
L. 2832
L. 2821
L. 2827
L. 2828

0   10 cm

L. 2822
L. 2823
L. 2829
L. 2824
L. 2833
L. 2820
L. 9140
L. 9141
L. 9148

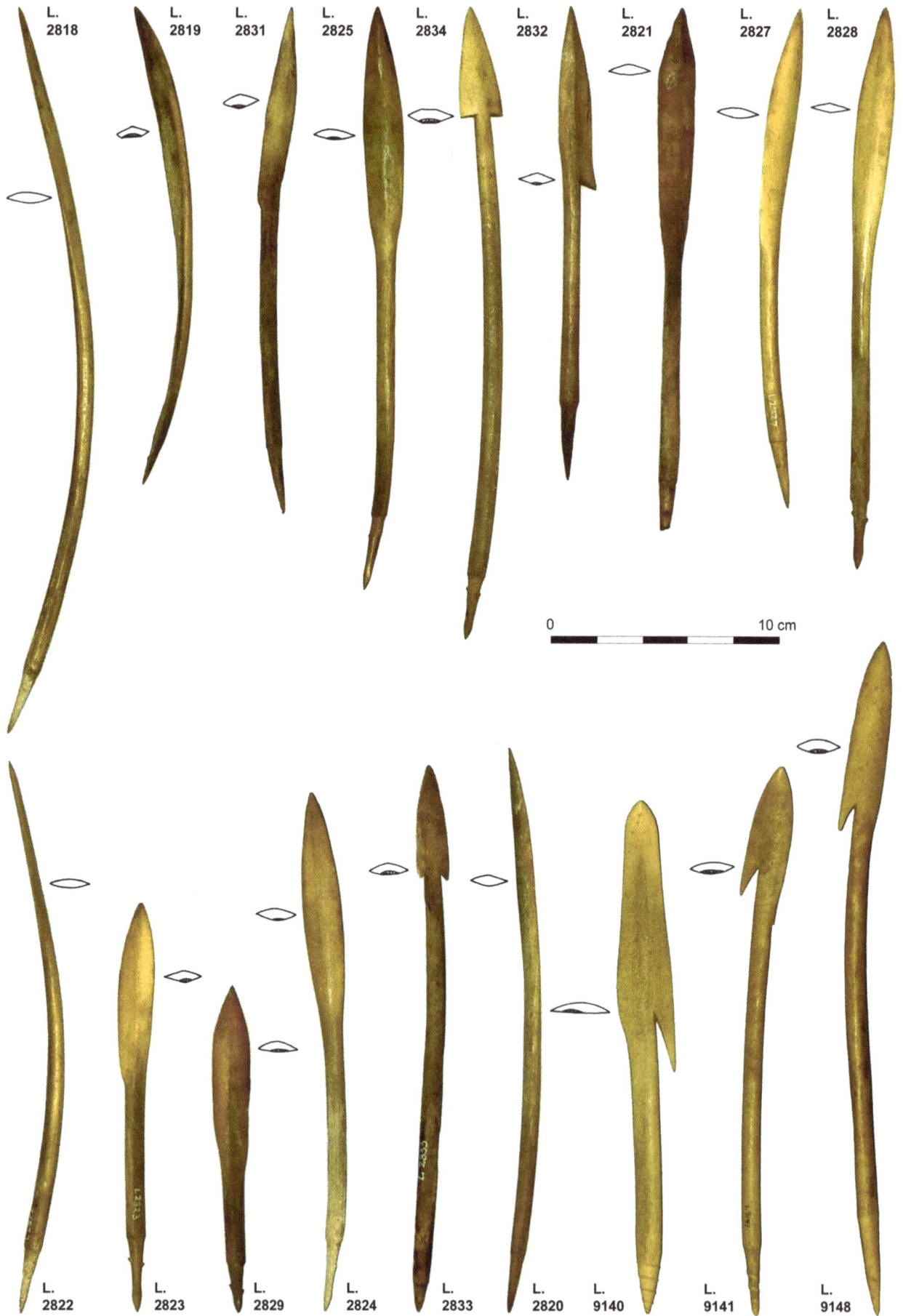

Plate 17. Antler arrow points from Disko Bay.

Lb. 194

Lc. 81

Lb. 232

0   20 cm

Plate 18. Bows from Central West Greenland.

Lb. 35

Lb. 233

Lb. 1

Lb. 190

0   20 cm

Plate 19. Bows from Central West Greenland.

Tip
- back

L 12.1952

Upper tip
- back

Lc. 81

Handle
- side

Handle

Lb. 190

Upper limb
- back

Lower limb
- belly

Upper tip
- back

Lb. 232

Handle

Upper limb
- back

Upper tip
- back

Lb. 233

Handle

Upper limb
- back

5 cm

Upper tip
- back

Lb. 194

Handle

Upper limb
- belly

0

Upper tip
- back

Lb. 35

Handle

Upper limb
- belly

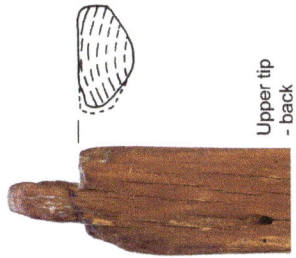

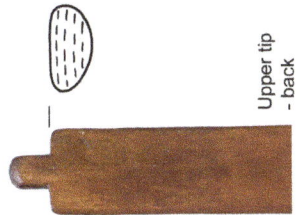

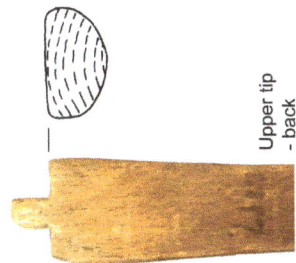

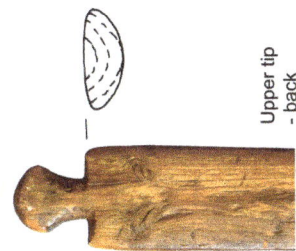

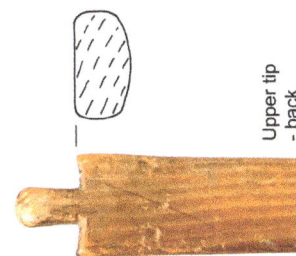

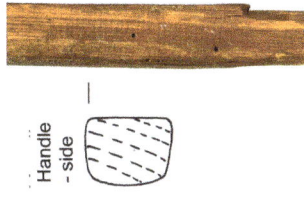

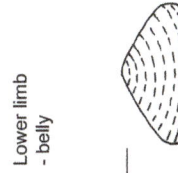

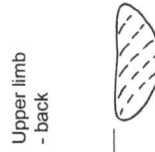

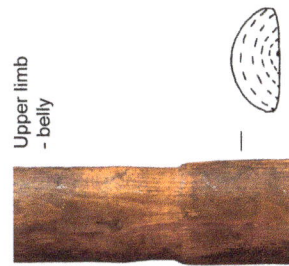

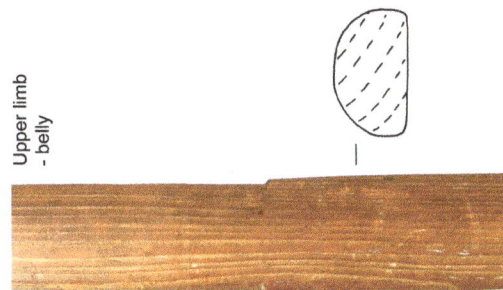

Plate 20. Bows from Central West Greenland – details.

53

side

back

belly

Upper tip

belly

**Upper
mid-limb**

side

**Upper rear end
- back**

0   5 cm

**Lower
mid-limb**

Handle

back

side

side

back

belly

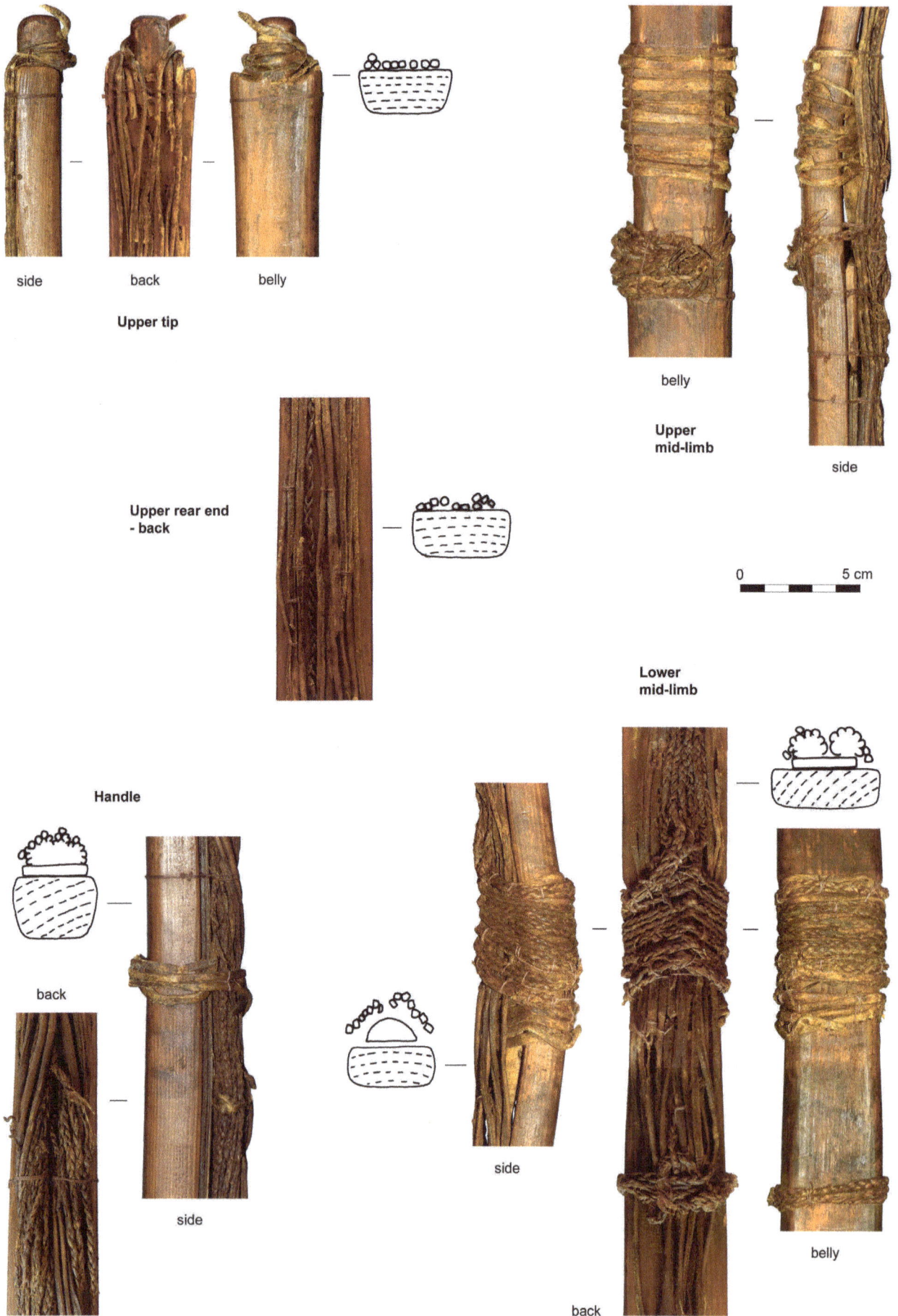

Plate 21. Central West Greenland: Kunstkammer bow Lb. 1.

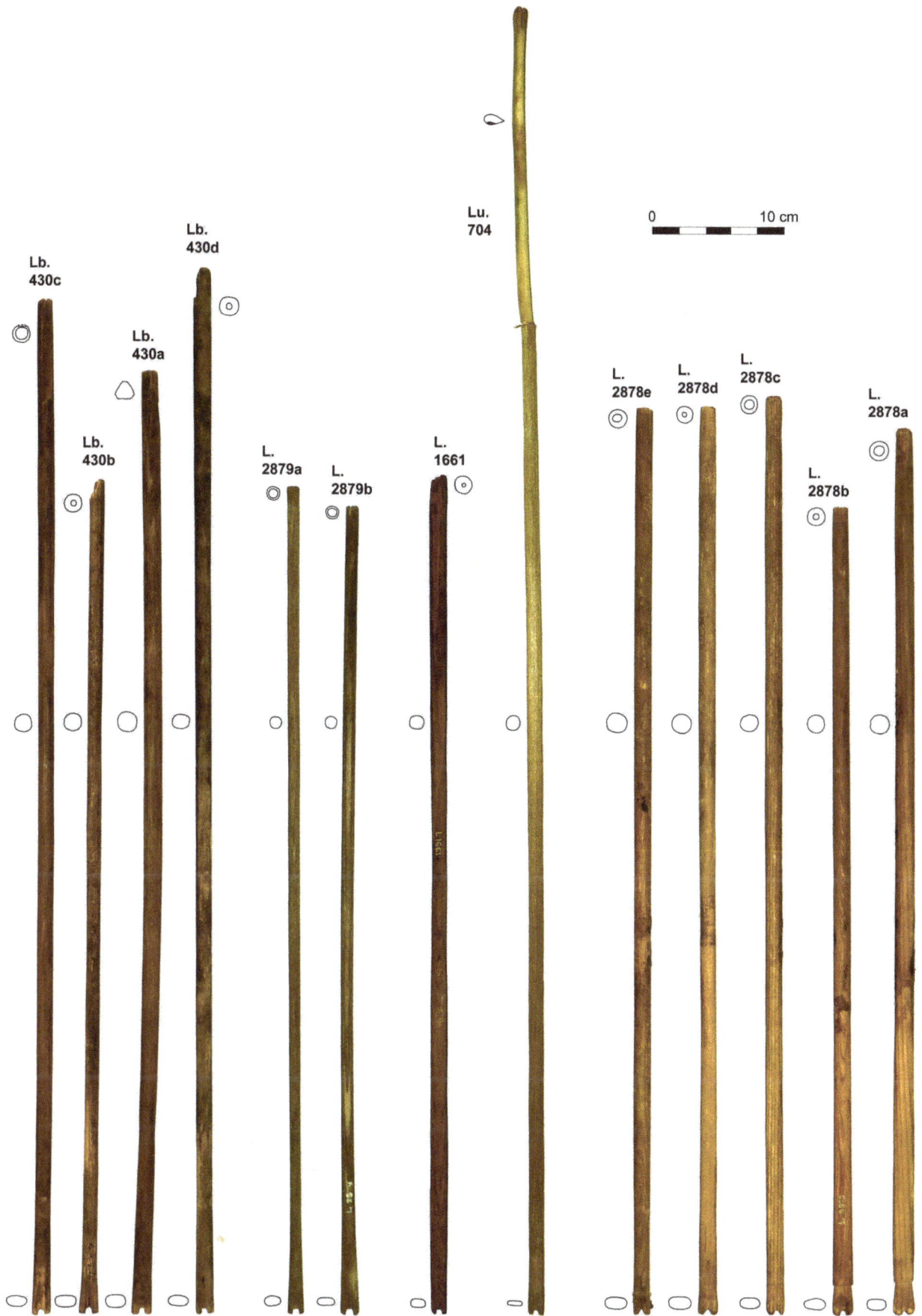

Plate 22. Arrows from Central West Greenland.

L 8.1956

L 8.1955

L 8.1954

L 8.1953

L 8.1839

L 8.1789

L. 5965

L. 2898

L 6.885

L 6.876

5 cm

0

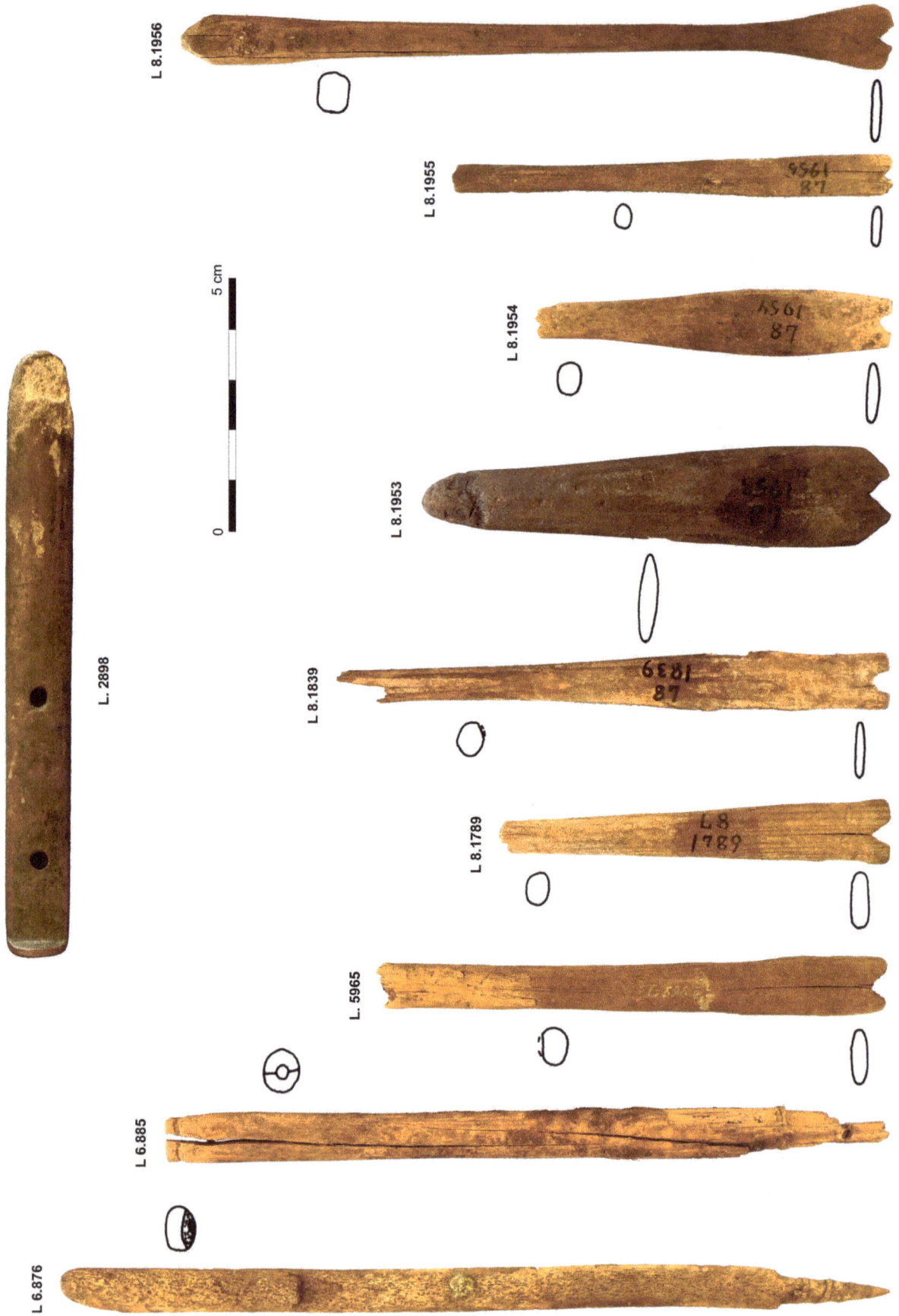

Plate 23. Arrows from Central West Greenland.

Distal end

Distal end

Distal end

Distal end

L. 2878e

L. 2878b

L. 2879b

L. 2878c

L. 2878d

Mid-shaft

Mid-shaft

0

5 cm

Distal end

Lb. 430d

Distal end

Distal end

Distal end

Mid-shaft

Lu. 704

Lb. 430a

Lb. 430b

Lb. 430c

Plate 24. Arrows from Central West Greenland – details.

57

L. 2860

L. 2877

L. 2876

L. 2874

L. 2875

Lb. 79

Lb. 54a

Lb. 54b

Lb. 55

L. 2869

0   10 cm

L. 1693

L. 1694

L. 1695a

L. 1695b

L. 1696

Plate 25. Antler foreshafts and arrow points from West Greenland.

L 1.4293

L. 3862

L. 3660

Lc. 1424

0   20 cm

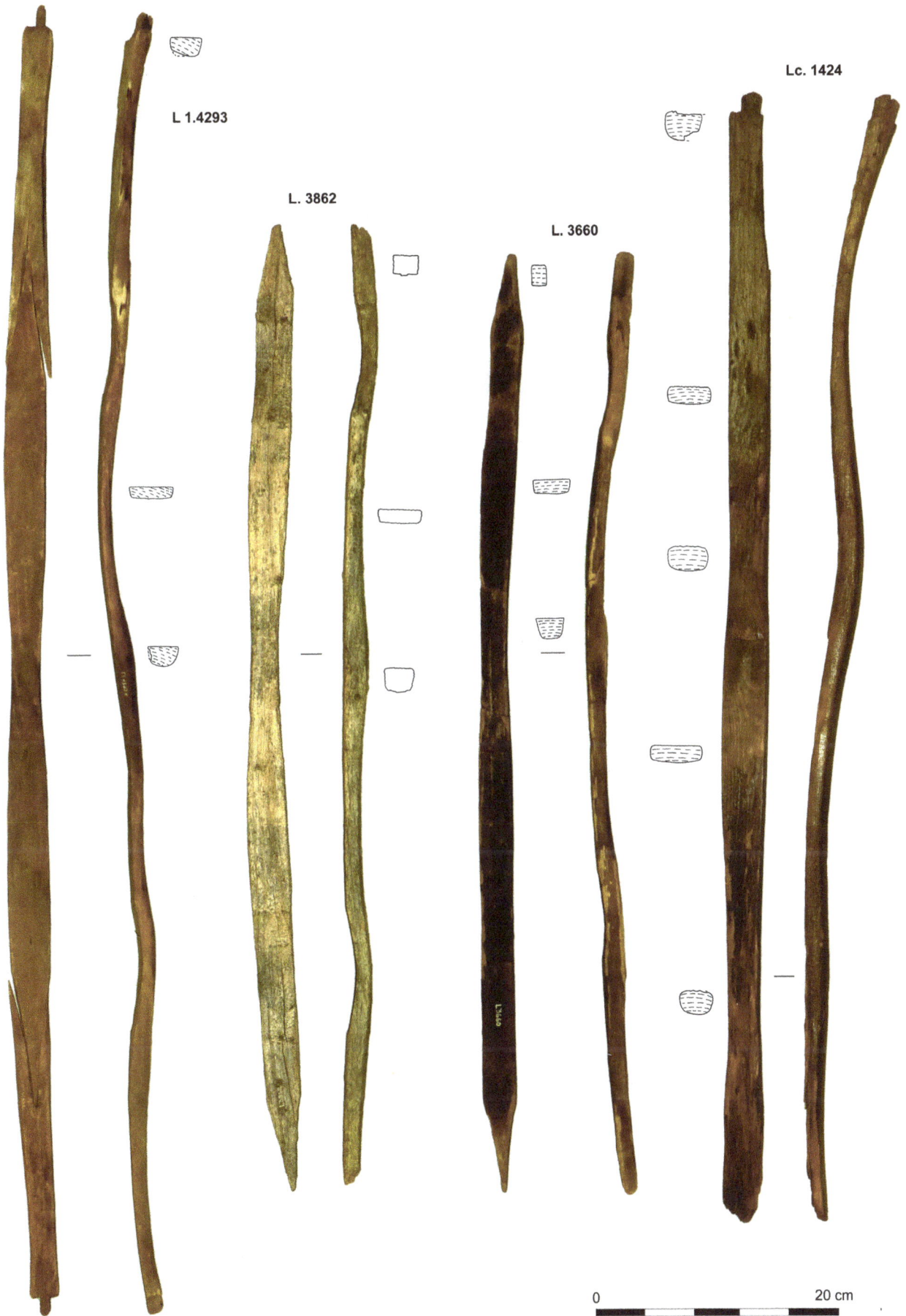

Plate 26. Bows from East Greenland.

L. 6617

L. 3661

L. 4059

L 1.4183

L 1.3527

L 1.4401

Schwach's
find

Plate 27. Bows from East Greenland.

Schwach's
find

Rear end
- side

Mid-limb - belly

L 1.4401

Rear end - back

0   5 cm

Lc. 1424

Tip - back

L. 5966

L. 4058

L 1.3867

0   5 cm

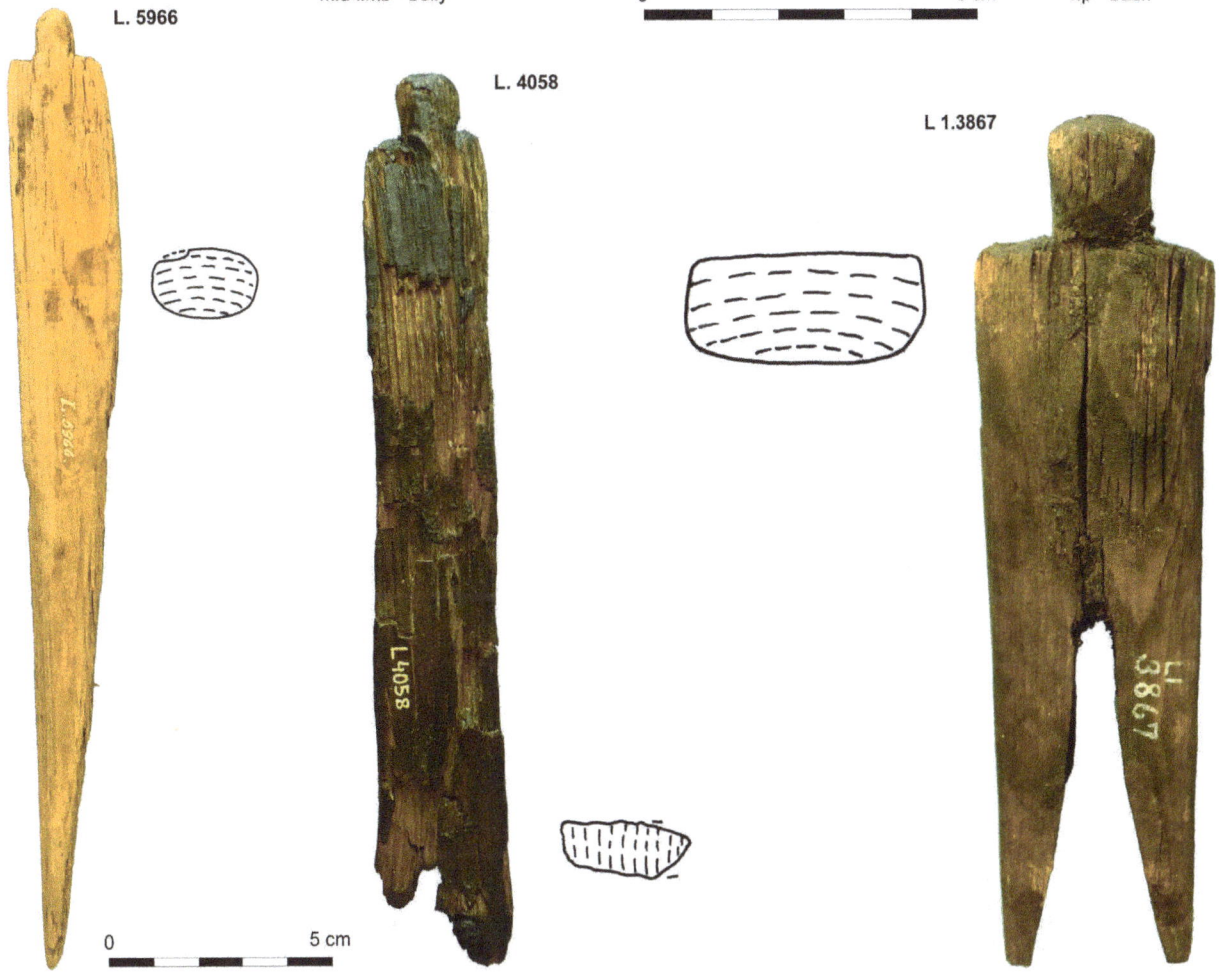

Plate 28. Bows from East Greenland – details.

61

L. 3663

10 cm

0

L 1.6657

Distal end

5 cm

0

Proximal end

Plate 29. Arrows from East Greenland.

L 3.11837

L 3.11838

L. 2245

L 8.2530

L 8.2531

L 8.2545

L 8.3286

West Greenland

10 cm

0

L 6.964

L 12.2019

L 12.1674

L. 3244

L 1.5909

L 1.3591

East Greenland

10 cm

0

L. 3439

L 1.3662

Plate 30. Miniature bows from West and East Greenland.

Plate 31. Four West Greenlanders. Oil painting 122 x 168 cm. Unknown artist. Bergen, 1654. National Museum of Denmark, Ethnographic Collection. Photograph Lennart Larsen. Reproduced courtesy of the National Museum of Denmark.

Plate 32. Qiperoq (left) and Pooq (right). Oil painting 126 x 186 cm. B. Grodtschilling. Copenhagen, 1724. National Museum of Denmark, Ethnographic Collection. Photographer unknown. Reproduced courtesy of the National Museum of Denmark.

Plate 33. Detail from Hans Egede's map *Nova Delineatio Grønlandiæ Antiqvæ* showing a fictional fighting scene between Norse and Greenlanders. Water colour. Copenhagen, 1737. Det Kgl. Bibliotek, Copenhagen. Reproduced courtesy of Det Kgl. Bibliotek.

Plate 34. The caribou hunt of Meqqisaalik. Water colour. Aaron of Kangeq. West Greenland, 1863. Greenland National Museum and Archives. Reproduced courtesy of the Greenland National Museum and Archives.

The Greenland bow in context

4.1. Bow design and use environment

As has been shown, the Greenland bow is not a homogeneous concept but features great regional variability. The different design traditions are necessarily linked with differences in performance, shooting behaviour and accuracy as well as handiness and ease of maintenance (Baker 1992). The bows and arrows from Central West and East Greenland tend to be long, allowing a full draw length of 60–70 cm, comparable to the weapons of the Copper Inuit in the beginning of the 20th century (Pl. 37). The same can be expected for the baleen bows from the northwest coast. A long bow of high draw weight with a corresponding draw length can cast a heavy arrow over a long distance (Junkmanns 2013, 45; tab. 9) and is also accurate because of its stability. The always very careful workmanship on the arrows from those regions reflects a pursuit of optimal flight behaviour and accuracy. From Central West Greenland, it is known that apart from the prevalent close-range blind hunting, stalking with greater shooting distances was also practiced (Fabricius 1818, 239; Grønnow et al. 1983, 20; 31; 83). To shoot musk ox or polar bear, both very tough prey species (Steensby 1910, 302), heavy arrows were required to ensure sufficient impact. Yet, a long hunting bow and a set of heavy arrows kept in a quiver-bow case combination are a considerable weight to be carried around and also quite bulky (comp. Jenness 1922, fig. 2.47): Hans Egede's son, Poul Egede (1790, 171 ff.) reports on an exhausting caribou hunting trip of several days in the inland of Nuuk Fjord, on which he accompanied a hunter who carried only his heavy quiver-bow case combination and a walking stick. In stark contrast, the short wood and antler bows from Northwest and Polar Greenland are designed for draw lengths of just 30–50 cm (comp. Malaurie 1990, 184) and therefore store much less energy, resulting in a considerably lower arrow speed. The tiny antler composite bows used by the early 20th century Netsilik on King William Land, strongly resembling those from the Thule region (Birket-Smith 1945, 48 f.), were ineffective against caribou at shooting distances over 20 m, a point at which accuracy also rapidly fell off (Balikci 1989, 42; Rasmussen 1926, 180; Stefánsson 1914, 96). In return, the shortness of these weapons resulted in high shooting frequency, ease of transport and great maneuverability, especially when shot from a kneeling position or from behind blinds (Pl. 35 and 36).

How strong were the Greenland bows? All traditional bow making cultures fashioned their archery equipment to precisely fit the proportions, strength and preferences of the individual (Baker 1994; Cattelain 1997; Roth 2004). Bows and arrows thus grew and shrank with their users during their lifetime. Consequently, the draw weights will always vary considerably. Nevertheless, the bow of an adult Greenlandic hunter must have been able to cast a heavy hunting arrow fast enough to kill a caribou or musk ox. The triple-curved wood composites of the Copper Inuit on Victoria Island were reported to frequently send the arrow completely through the body of a full-grown caribou at distances of as much as 40 meters (Stefánsson 1914, 96). The maximum shooting distance with a heavy hunting arrow was around 120 meters (Jenness 1922, 146). The Greenland bows Lb. 35, Lb. 1, and Lc. 1424 (Pl. 19 and 26) doubtlessly were such strong hunting bows, whereas Lc. 232 and L 1.4293 (Pl. 18 and 26) probably have been weapons used by adolescents. An old ethnographic museum specimen from Alaska with a wooden stave, simple d-profile and Arctic cable backing was tested by Saxton Pope (1923, 338) and still drew an impressive 80 lbs at 66 cm when tested, casting a light arrow 164 meters. Modern reconstructions can also help to estimate the draw weights of Arctic bows, although the results will always be biased by the considerable variability of the mechanical properties of biological raw materials (Junkmanns 2013, 63 f.) For example, the replica of a typical antler composite bow from the Thule region made by bowyer Flemming Alrune drew only 40 lbs (Baker 1994, 86). That kind of bow was of no use against musk ox and polar bear (Steensby 1910, 302).

4.2. Shooting technique

All across the Arctic, the so-called 'Mediterranean' release seems to have been applied with the index finger above the flattened arrow nock and the middle and sometimes also the ring finger below (Birket-Smith 1918, 10; 1929, 106; 1948, 117; Hamilton 1982, fig. 30; Jenness 1946, 126; Malaurie 1990, 184; Mathiassen 1945, 58; Rasmussen 1926, 180; Steensby 1910, 357). The bow itself was held perpendicular or diagonal in the left hand with the arrow to the left side in the case of a right-handed archer (Birket-Smith 1918, 10; Jenness 1946, 126; Mathiassen 1945, 56) (Pl. 35–37). According to the archaeological and ethnographic evidence, the Greenland Thule archers did not use wrist guards to protect the bow arm from the snapping string. As Arctic bows were often braced quite high and their users frequently wore long-sleeved cloths and even mittens (Pl. 37), wrist guards were possibly regarded as unnecessary. Yet, the Copper Inuit occasionally used small oval osseous wrist guards (Birket-Smith 1945, Fig. 3.51; Jenness 1946, 132; fig. 170).

4.3. Bow hunting strategies

In principle, there were two different bow hunting strategies in the North American Arctic: solitary stalking and the communal hunt. The main prey species was always the caribou (Birket-Smith 1929, 106 ff.; 1945, 48; Gordon 1990; Grønnow et al. 1983, 26 ff.; Jenness 1922, 146 ff.; Mathiassen 1945, 53 ff.; Pasda 2011, 47 ff.; Steensby 1910, 303 f.). The stalking hunt was performed by individuals or small groups and required a lot of patience and knowledge to get close enough to the prey for a precise shot. Thus, imitations of typical animal characteristics like appearance, movements and noises were brought to perfection (Binford 2009, 215; Birket-Smith 1945, 48; Jenness 1922, 146; Mathiassen 1945, 54; Steensby 1910, 303). This hunting technique was typically applied, when the caribou populations were at a minimum (Pasda 2011, 49).

The communal hunt, on the other hand, was the most important and productive method until the gun replaced the bow (Petersen 2003, 140). In West Greenland, the great summer hunts were preeminent events in the annual life cycle. Big inland settlements for exploiting the migrating caribou herds, like Aasivissuit in the Sisimiut region, played a key role for social interaction and exchange amongst West Greenland Thule populations (Grønnow et al. 1983, 16). It is possible that the communal caribou summer hunt was a defining feature of the Greenland Thule culture from the very beginning (Gulløv 1997, 344 f.; Pasda 2011, 79). The main period of activity, however, seems to have been in the decades around 1700 AD when the West Greenland caribou population was at a maximum (Grønnow 2009, 201; Pasda 2011, 54). The hunt itself was typically carried out as an organised battue with many participants (Grønnow et al. 1983, 27; Petersen 2003, 140). The principle applied was always more or less the same (Grønnow et al. 1983, 17 ff.; Egede 1741, 335; Fabricius 1818, 239; Grønnow 2009, 201): The beaters, mostly women and children, surrounded the caribou and chased them towards the archers hiding behind stone-built shooting blinds – called *tellut* – often being located at topographic bottleneck situations. For shooting from behind their blinds, the archers either stood, possibly with their feet and backs braced against big boulders for more stability (Grønnow et al. 1983, 29), or they kneeled (Pl. 35). The arrows were released at close range and the objective was to kill or wound as many animals as possible before the quiver was empty (Binford 2009, 215) (Pl. 34). To further enhance the channelling of the caribou herds during the communal hunt, long rows of stone cairns – *inussuit* – or wooden poles with a sod on top were built at favourable topographic situations and equipped with strings and flapping bird wings (Grønnow et al. 1983, fig. 39; 45; 2009, 205). Being witnesses of the big summer hunts that contributed so much to the identity of the Thule Inuit, the summer camps and associated hunting drives are outstanding features of the Greenland cultural landscape (Grønnow 2009, 201; Pasda 2011, 77; UNESCO 1557).

The communal hunts with a considerable number of participants doubtlessly required some sort of identification of the individual archers (Petersen 2003, 141). In 1926, the West Greenland hunter Jens Rosing stated that in the old days, different numbers and positions of barbs on the osseous arrowheads served as owner's marks (Grønnow et al. 1983, 30). Could that have been an option? First, a great many arrowheads, especially from Northwest and East Greenland, totally lack barbs or have only a single one (Fig. 3.7; Pl. 17). In these cases, a function as owner's marks can be excluded. Second, the elaborate Greenland antler arrowheads in analogy to the barbed points of the European late Upper Palaeolithic and the North American Tlingit harpoons (Weniger 1987) very likely have a complex biography, constantly changing their shape due to frequent reworking after damage. Apart from getting progressively shorter, a reduced number of barbs are to be expected, resulting in quite heterogeneous arrowhead sets. Consequently there is not one single identical pair of arrowheads in the studied material (comp. Pl. 17 and 25). Two grave inventories from West Greenland presented by Porsild (1915b, pl. III) feature a great deal of variability as well. And among the Copper Inuit and Netsilik, arrows from the same set usually had very different heads (Birket-Smith 1945, fig. 19 a–d; Stefánsson 1914, fig. 33). All these observations speak for scepticism towards Rosing's statement but of course, the lack of geminate arrowheads from Greenland might be due to find context (see 3.1.). A solution to the question of owner's marks thus cannot be offered here. But taking the examples of 19th century North American Plains societies (Bohr 2000, 46 f.) and the Canadian ice patches (Alix et al. 2012), shaft painting and different fletching styles can also be expected to act as individual markers.

Plate 35. Netsilik practising archery. King William Land, Fifth Thule Expedition 1921–1924. National Museum of Denmark, Ethnographic Collection. Photographer unknown. Reproduced courtesy of the National Museum of Denmark.

Plate 36. Netsilik practising archery. King William Land, Fifth Thule Expedition 1921–1924. National Museum of Denmark, Ethnographic Collection. Photographer unknown. Reproduced courtesy of the National Museum of Denmark.

Plate 37. Copper Inuit archers. Minto Inlet, Northwest Territories, Canada. Photograph by George Wilkins or John Hadley, 19 May 1916 during the Canadian Arctic Expedition 1913–1918. Canadian Museum of History, Photograph Archives. Reproduced courtesy of the Canadian Museum of History.

5

Conclusion and perspectives

Archery equipment was an essential part of the toolkit of the Greenland Thule culture. From the very beginning, the bow had been the primary weapon for hunting land mammals and kept that role until it was replaced by firearms during the 18th and 19th centuries.

The Greenland bow is characterised by a high degree of variability – not so much from a chronological but certainly from a regional point of view. The key factor seems to be the abundance of suitable raw materials. It is readily apparent that in regions with a good supply of driftwood self bow staves were made, whereas composite staves dominated where it was scarce. The case of the laminated baleen bow from Northwest Greenland shows the readiness to exploit particular local resources. Both design and technology of Greenland archery equipment mirror holarctic Thule traditions. This holds true for silhouettes, profiles and cross sections as well as for joining techniques and backing types. However, some features are distinctively Greenlandic. Possibly the most prominent example is the screw tang that seems to have emerged autochthonously from the knob tang sometime during the 15th century in Northeast and the 16th century in West Greenland. Other examples are the long d-bows with shoulders from Central West Greenland and the shallow East Greenland triple-curved bow profiles that were carved and not heat bent. Like their western neighbours, the Greenland Inuit made intensive use of the bow and arrow to hunt caribou. The big communal hunts during its population maxima played an important role for subsistence and social interaction.

It has also become obvious how quickly the complex Thule archery technology fell into oblivion. Be it ethnographic models from Polar Greenland, or statements of local informants in the case of West Greenland: As soon as the bow and arrow stopped being made and used in daily life the specific knowhow connected to them began to erode. Just one generation seems to have been enough to make information on both technology and application of the weapon unreliable. Thus, the great scepticism early scholars like H. P. Steensby show to such 'secondary' ethnographic sources is justified. There are many perspectives for future work. Concerning the find material itself, detailed wood analyses (e.g. Alix 2009) could state the macroscopic observations on wood species and quality more precisely. For example, the compression wood hypothesis could be tested this way. Moreover, direct dating of selected diagnostic types could help to refine the chronological framework of Greenland archery. This is particularly true for osseous arrowheads as these artefacts seem to be very good spatial-chronological markers. From the technological point of view, faithful reconstructions of different Arctic bow and arrow types and comparative shooting experiments would allow statements as to operation chain, time factor, energy storage capacity and efficiency. Especially the distinctive and enigmatic triple-curved bow design should be assessed.

Doubtlessly, the Arctic bow has its cultural and technological roots in Asia (Cattelain 1997, 31; Grayson 1993, 153; Hamilton 1982, 70 ff.). The Neolithic Old Bering Sea culture used typical Central Asian composite bows with spliced-in osseous *siyahs* (Leskov and Müller-Beck 1993, 126), and the Palaeo-Inuit Ipiutak culture in Alaska seems to have applied the bow and arrow even as their main weapon system (Larsen and Rainey 1948, 63 ff.) The Punuk culture, a direct forerunner of the Thule tradition, seems to have used the bow primarily for warfare (Bandi 1995, 170; fig. 2.6), hence reflecting a distinct Asian tradition (Bergman and McEwen 1997, 158). However, we do not yet know exactly how the diffusion of archery from Asia to the Arctic proceeded, neither from a chronological nor technological point of view (Lepola 2015). To make progress here, further studies should be conducted in the other Arctic regions, taking into account archaeological and ethnographic objects as well as written sources from the Eastern and Central Arctic, Alaska, and Siberia. On this basis, it should eventually be possible to reconstruct the transformation process from a primarily martial weapon to a dedicated hunting tool. Main questions could address the origin of the cable backing and its formal diversity, the emergence of the triple-curved bow design and the social role of archery in both conflicts and communal hunts. Because of its widespread occurrence, high chronological sensitivity, and strong regional variability, archery equipment has always been – and continues to be – a prime source for Arctic cultural studies.

References

Allely and Hamm 2002: S. Allely and J. Hamm, Encyclopedia of Native American bows, arrows and quivers – Vol. 2 (Goldthwaite 2002).

Alix 2001: C. Alix, Exploitation du bois par les populations néoeskimo entre le nord de l'Alaska et le Haut Arctique canadien. PhD thesis, Université de Paris I – Panthéon Sorbonne (Paris 2001).

Alix 2009: C. Alix, Driftwood, timber and shrubs! Wood used by Ruin Islander Thule at Skraeling Island, eastern Ellesmere Island, Canada. In: B. Grønnow (Ed.), On the track of the Thule culture from Bering Strait to East Greenland. Proceedings of the SILA conference "The Thule culture – New perspectives in Inuit prehistory" Copenhagen, Oct. 26th–28th, 2006. Papers in honor of Hans Christian Gulløv (Copenhagen 2009) 149–165.

Alix et al. 2012: C. Alix / P. G. Hare / T. D. Andrews / G. McKay, A thousand years of lost hunting arrows: Wood analysis of ice patch remains in Northwestern Canada. Arctic 65, suppl. 1, 2012, 95–117.

Amdrup 1902: G. Amdrup, Carlsbergfondets Expedition til Øst-Grønland, udført i Aarene 1898–1900 under Ledelse af G. Amdrup. Meddeleser om Grønland 27 (Copenhagen 1902).

Appelt 2005: M. Appelt, De sidste Dorsetfolk. In: H. C. Gulløv (Ed.), Grønlands forhistorie (Copenhagen ²2005) 177–200.

Appelt and Gulløv 1999: M. Appelt and H. C. Gulløv (Eds), Late Dorset in High Arctic Greenland. Final report on the Gateway to Greenland project (Copenhagen 1999).

Arneborg 2005: J. Arneborg, Det europæiske landnam – Nordboerne i Grønland. In: H. C. Gulløv (Ed.), Grønlands forhistorie (Copenhagen ²2005) 219–278.

Baker 1992: T. Baker, Bow design and performance. In: J. Hamm (Ed.), The traditional bowyer's bible – Vol. 1 (New York 1992) 43–116.

Baker 1993: T. Baker, Bows from boards. In: J. Hamm (Ed.), The traditional bowyer's bible – Vol. 2 (New York 1993) 19–50.

Baker 1994: T. Baker, Bows of the world. In: J. Hamm (Ed.), The traditional bowyer's bible – Vol. 3 (New York 1994) 43–98.

Balikci 1989: A. Balikci, The Netsilik Eskimo (Prospect Heights 1989).

Bandi 1965: H.-G. Bandi, Urgeschichte der Eskimo (Stuttgart 1965).

Bandi 1995: H.-G. Bandi, Siberian Eskimos as whalers and warriors. In: A. P. McCartney (Ed.), Hunting the largest animals. Native whaling in the Western Arctic and Subarctic. Studies in Whaling – Vol. 3 (Alberta 1995) 165–183.

Bartlett 1931: R. Bartlett, The Bartlett East Greenland expedition. Geographical Review 21, 1931, 398–414.

Barton and Bergman 1982: R. N. E. Barton and C. A. Bergman, Hunters at Hengistbury. Some evidence from experimental archaeology. World Archaeology 14, 1982, 237–248.

Beckhoff 1963: K. Beckhoff, Die Eibenholz-Bogen vom Ochsenmoor am Dümmer. Die Kunde – Neue Forschungen 14, 1963, 63–81.

Beckhoff 1965: K. Beckhoff, Eignung und Verwendung einheimischer Holzarten für prähistorische Pfeilschäfte. Die Kunde – Neue Forschungen 16, 1965, 51–61.

Bergman and McEwen 1997: C. A. Bergman and E. McEwen, Sinew-reinforced and composite bows – technology, function, and social implications. In: H. Knecht (Ed.), Projectile technology (New York 1997) 143–160.

Bergman et al. 1988: C. A. Bergman / E. McEwen / R. Miller, Experimental archery: projectile velocities and comparison of bow performances. Antiquity 62, 1988, 658–670.

Binford 2009: L. R. Binford, Nunamiut subsistence provinces – the mountain area: Hunting with bow versus gun. In: B. Grønnow (Ed.), On the track of the Thule culture from Bering Strait to East Greenland. Proceedings of the SILA conference "The Thule culture – New perspectives in Inuit prehistory" Copenhagen, Oct. 26th–28th, 2006. Papers in honor of Hans Christian Gulløv (Copenhagen 2009) 211–222.

Birket-Smith 1918: K. Birket-Smith, The Greenland bow. Meddelelser om Grønland 56/1 (Copenhagen 1918).

Birket-Smith 1929: K. Birket-Smith, The Caribou Eskimos. Material culture and social life and their cultural position. Report of the Fifth Thule Expedition – Vol. 5 (Copenhagen 1929).

Birket-Smith 1945: K. Birket-Smith, Ethnographical collections from the Northwest Passage. Report of the Fifth Thule Expedition – Vol. 6/2 (Copenhagen 1945).

Birket-Smith 1948: K. Birket-Smith, Die Eskimos (Zürich 1948).

Boas 1901: F. Boas, The Eskimo of Baffin Land and Hudson Bay. Bulletin of the American Museum of Natural History 15/1, 1901, 1–370.

Boas 1907: F. Boas, Second report on the Eskimo of Baffin Land and Hudson Bay. Bulletin of the American Museum of Natural History 15/2, 1907, 371–570.

Bohr 1998: R. Bohr, Pfeil und Bogen der Plains- und Prärieindianer Nordamerikas (Wyk 1998).

Bohr 2000: R. Bohr, Pfeilmacher und Bogentänzer – Kulturelle und gesellschaftliche Aspekte des Bogenschießens der Plains- und Prärieindianer (Wyk 2000).

Buchwald 2001: V. F. Buchwald, Ancient iron and slags in Greenland. Meddelelser om Grønland, Man and Society 26 (Copenhagen 2001).

Bugge 1930: G. N. Bugge, John Davis tre rejser til Grønland i aarene 1585–87. Det Grønlandske Selskabs Skrifter 7, 1930, 1–95.

Callahan 2001: E. Callahan, Archery in the Arctic. In: D. Wescott (Ed.), Primitive technology – Vol. 2. Ancestral skills (Layton 2001) 119–133.

Cattelain 1997: P. Cattelain, Hunting during the Upper Paleolithic: Bow, spearthrower, or both? In: H. Knecht (Ed.), Projectile technology (New York 1997) 213–240.

Chen et al. 2008: P.-Y. Chen / A. Y. M. Lin / Y.-S. Lin / Y. Seki / A. G. Stokes / J. Peyras / E. A. Olevsky / M. A. Meyers / J. McKittrick, Structure and mechanical properties of selected biological materials. Journal of the Mechanical Behavior of Biomedical Materials 1, 2008, 208–226.

Comstock 1992: P. Comstock, Other backings. In: J. Hamm (Ed.), The traditional bowyer's bible – Vol. 1 (New York 1992) 233–256.

Comstock 1993a: P. Comstock, Bending wood. In: J. Hamm (Ed.), The traditional bowyer's bible – Vol. 2 (New York 1993) 155–166.

Comstock 1993b: P. Comstock, Ancient European bows. In: J. Hamm (Ed.), The traditional bowyer's bible – Vol. 2 (New York 1993) 81–102.

Cranz 1770: D. Cranz, Historie von Grönland – Vol 1 (Barby / Leipzig 1770).

Damas 1984: D. Damas, Copper Eskimo. In: D. Damas (Ed.), Handbook of North American Indians – Vol. 5 (Washington 1984), 397–141.

Egede 1741: H. Egede, Relationer fra Grønland 1721–36 og Det gamle Grønlands ny Perlustration 1741. Ed. L. Bobé. Meddelelser om Grønland 54 (Copenhagen 1925).

Egede 1790: P. Egede, Nachrichten aus Grönland. Aus einem Tagebuche, geführt von 1721 bis 1788 (Copenhagen 1790).

Elmer 1952: R. P. Elmer, Target archery (London 1952).

Fabricius 1818: O. Fabricius, Nøiagtig beskrivelse over Grønlandernes landdyr-, fugle- og fiskefangst med dertil hørende redskaber (Copenhagen 1818).

Farbregd 2009: O. Farbregd, Archery history from ancient snow and ice. In: T. Brattli (Ed.), The 58th International Sachsensymposium, 1–5 September 2007. Vitark 7, Acta Archaeologica Nidrosiensia (Trondheim 2009) 157–170.

Fienup-Riordan 2007: A. Fienup-Riordan, Yuungnaqpiallerput – The way we genuinely live. Masterworks of Yup'ik Science and Survival (Seattle / London 2007).

Friesen and Arnold 2008: T. M. Friesen and C. D. Arnold, The Timing of the Thule Migration: New Dates from the Western Canadian Arctic. American Anitquity 73/3, 2008, 527–538.

Giddings and Anderson 1986: J. L. Giddings and D. D. Anderson, Beach ridge archaeology of Cape Krusenstern. Eskimo and pre-Eskimo settlements around Kotzebue Sound, Alaska (Washington DC 1986).

Glahn 1771: H. C. Glahn, Anmærkninger over de tre første Bøger af Hr. David Crantzes Historie om Grønland (Copenhagen 1771).

Glob 1935: P. V. Glob, Eskimo settlements in Kempe fjord and King Oskar fjord. Meddelelser om Grønland 102/2 (Copenhagen 1935).

Glob 1946: P. V. Glob, Eskimo settlements in Northeast Greenland. Meddelelser om Grønland 144/6 (Copenhagen 1946).

Gordon 1990: B. C. Gordon, World rangifer communal hunting. In: L. B. Davis and B. O. K. Reeves (Eds), Hunters of the recent past (London 1990) 277–303.

Grayson 1993: C. E. Grayson, Composite bows. In: J. Hamm (Ed.), The traditional bowyer's bible – Vol. 2 (New York 1993) 113–154.

Grønnow 1996: B. Grønnow, Driftwood and Saqqaq culture woodworking in West Greenland. In: B. Jacobsen / C. Andreasen / J. Rygaard (Eds), Cultural and social research in Greenland 95/96 – Essays in honor of Robert Petersen (Nuuk 1996) 73–89.

Grønnow 2009: B. Grønnow, Caribou hunting structures and hunting grounds of the Thule culture in Angujaarturfiup Nunaa, West Greenland. In: B. Grønnow (Ed.), On the track of the Thule culture from Bering Strait to East Greenland. Proceedings of the SILA conference "The Thule culture – New perspectives in Inuit prehistory" Copenhagen, Oct. 26th–28th, 2006. Papers in honor of Hans Christian Gulløv (Copenhagen 2009) 201–210.

Grønnow 2010: B. Grønnow, The history of archaeological research in North East Greenland: Putting the GeoArk project into perspective. Geografisk Tidsskrift – Danish Journal of Geography 110/2, 2010, 117–129.

Grønnow and Jensen 2003: B. Grønnow and J. Fog Jensen, The northernmost ruins of the globe – Eigil Knuth's archaeological investigations in Peary Land and adjacent areas of high Arctic Greenland. Monographs on Greenland, Man and Society 29 (Copenhagen 2003).

Grønnow et al. 1983: B. Grønnow / M. Meldgaard / J. Berglund Nielsen, Aasivissuit – The Great Summer Camp. Archaeological, ethnological and zoo-archaeological studies of a caribou-hunting site in West Greenland. Meddelelser om Grønland, Man and Society 5 (Odense 1983).

Gulløv 1997: H. C. Gulløv, From middle ages to colonial times – Archaeological and ethnohistorical studies of the Thule culture in South West Greenland 1300–1800 AD. Meddelelser om Grønland, Man and Society 23 (Copenhagen 1997).

Gulløv 2005: H. C. Gulløv, Nunarput, vort land – Thulekulturen. In: H. C. Gulløv (Ed.), Grønlands forhistorie (Copenhagen ²2005) 281–343.

Gulløv 2009: H. C. Gulløv, Douglas Charles Claverings beretning fra Nordøstgrønland 1823. Tidskriftet Grønland 57, 2009, 108–125.

Gulløv 2016: H. C. Gulløv, Inuit-European interactions in Greenland. In: T. M. Friesen and O. K. Mason (Eds), The Oxford handbook of the prehistoric Arctic, chapter 38 (Oxford 2016) 897–914.

Gundestrup 1991: B. Gundestrup, Det kongelige danske Kunstkammer 1737 (Copenhagen 1991).

Hamilton 1982: T. M. Hamilton, Native American bows. Missouri Archaeological Society Special Publications 5 (Columbia 1982).

Hamm 1991: J. Hamm, Bows and Arrows of the Native Americans (Guilford 1991).

Hamm 1992: J. Hamm, Tillering. In: J. Hamm (Ed.), The traditional bowyer's bible – Vol. 1 (New York 1992) 257–286.

Hansen 1998: K. Hansen, Nuussuarmiut – hunting families on the big headland. Meddelelser om Grønland, Man and Society 35 (Viborg 2008).

Hardenberg 2009: M. Hardenberg, In search of Thule children: Miniature playthings as a means of socializing children. MA thesis. Department of Archaeology, Memorial University of Newfoundland (St. John`s 2009).

https://research.library.mun.ca/8798/1/Hardenberg_Mariane.pdf

Hardy 2006: R. Hardy, Longbow: A social and military history (Gloucestershire 2006).

Hickman et al. 1947: C. N. Hickmann / P. E. Klopsteg / F. Nagler, Archery: The technical side (Milwaukee 1947).

Higgins 2010: A. K. Higgins, Exploration history and place names of northern East Greenland. Geological Survey of Denmark and Greenland Bulletin 21 (Copenhagen 2010).

Holtved 1944: E. Holtved, Archaeological investigations in the Thule district – Vol. 1 and 2. Meddelelser om Grønland 141/1 and 2 (Copenhagen 1944).

Holtved 1954: E. Holtved, Archaeological investigations in the Thule district – Vol. 3. Meddelelser om Grønland 141/3 (Copenhagen 1954).

Holtved 1962: E. Holtved, Otto Fabricius' ethnographical works. Meddelelser om Grønland 140/2 (Copenhagen 1962).

Insulander 1999: R. Insulander, Den samiska pilbågen rekonstruerad: En jämførande analys av fynd från Sverige, Norge och Finland. Fornvännen 94, 1999, 73–87.

Insulander 2002: R. Insulander, The two-wood bow. Acta Borealia 1, 2002, 49–73.

Iovita and Sano 2016: R. Iovita and K. Sano (Eds), Multidisciplinary approaches to the study of Stone Age weaponry (New York 2016).

Jenness 1922: D. Jenness, The life of the Copper Eskimos – Southern party 1913–16. Report of the Canadian Arctic Expedition 7 (Ottawa 1922).

Jenness 1946: D. Jenness, Material culture of the Copper Eskimo – Southern party 1913–16. Report of the Canadian Arctic Expedition 16 (Ottawa 1946).

Junkmanns 2013: J. Junkmanns, Pfeil und Bogen – Von der Altsteinzeit bis zum Mittelalter (Ludwigshafen 2013).

Karpowicz 2007: A. Karpowicz, Ottoman bows – an assessment of draw weight, performance and tactical use. Antiquity 81, 2007, 675–685.

Kenyon and Arnold 1985: D. Kenyon and C. Arnold, Toys as indicators of socialization in Thule culture. In: Archaeological Association of the University of Calgary (Ed.), Proceedings of the 16th Annual Chacmool Conference: Status, structure and stratification: Current archaeological reconstructions (Calgary 1985) 347–353.

Kleinschmidt 1871: S. Kleinschmidt, Den Grønlandske ordbog (Copenhagen 1871).

Klopsteg 1947: P. E. Klopsteg, Turkish archery and the composite bow (Evanston 1947).

Knuth 1952: E. Knuth, An outline of the archaeology of Peary Land. Arctic 5/1, 1952, 17–33.

Knuth 1981: E. Knuth, Greenland news from between 81° and 83° North. Folk 23, 1981, 91–112.

Kooi 1991: B. W. Kooi, On the mechanics of the modern working-recurve bow. Computational Mechanics 8, 1991, 291–304.

Kooi and Bergman 1997: B. W. Kooi and C. A. Bergman, An approach to the study of ancient archery using mathematical modelling. Antiquity 71, 1997, 124–134.

Koppedrayer 2004: K. Koppedrayer, Cultural signatures: Bows from the Lakota nation. Journal of Archer Antiquaries 47 (South Gloucestershire 2004).

Langley 2016: M. Langley (Ed.), Osseous projectile weaponry. Towards an understanding of Pleistocene cultural variability (New York 2016).

Larsen 1934: H. Larsen, Dødemandsbugten – An Eskimo settlement on Clavering Island. Meddelelser om Grønland 102/1 (Copenhagen 1934).

Larsen and Rainey 1948: H. Larsen and F. Rainey, Ipiutak and the Arctic whale hunting culture. Anthropological Papers of The American Museum of Natural History 42 (New York 1948).

Lave and Wenger 1991: J. Lave and E. Wenger (Eds), Situated learning: Legitimate peripheral participation (Cambridge / New York 1991).

Lepers and Rots 2020: C. Lepers and V. Rots, The important role of bow choice and arrow fletching in projectile experimentation. A ballistic approach. Journal of Archaeological Science: Reports 34 (2020). https://doi.org/10.1016/j.jasrep.2020.102613

Lepola 2015: M. Lepola, Arctic bowyery – The use of compression wood in bows in the Subarctic and Arctic regions of Eurasia and America. Journal of Ethnology and Folkloristics 9/1, 2015, 41–60.

Leskov and Müller-Beck 1993: A. M. Leskov and H. Müller-Beck (Eds), Arktische Waljäger vor 3000 Jahren. Unbekannte sibirische Kunst (Mayence / Munich 1993).

Malaurie 1990: J. Malaurie, Ultima Thule (Paris 1990).

Margaris 2009: A. V. Margaris, The mechanical properties of marine and terrestrial skeletal Materials. Ethnoarchaeology 1/2, 2009, 163–184.

Margaris 2014: A. V. Margaris, Reconsidering raw material selection – Skeletal technologies and design for durability in Subarctic Alaska. Journal of Archaeological Method and Theory 21/3, 2014, 669–695.

Mason and Bowers 2009: O. K. Mason and P. M. Bowers, The origin of Thule is always elsewhere: Early Thule within Kotzebue Sound, 'Cul-de-sac' or nursery? In: B. Grønnow (Ed.), On the track of the Thule culture from Bering Strait to East Greenland. Proceedings of the SILA conference "The Thule culture – New perspectives in Inuit prehistory" Copenhagen, Oct. 26th–28th, 2006. Papers in honor of Hans Christian Gulløv (Copenhagen 2009) 25–44.

Mathiassen 1927a: T. Mathiassen, Archaeology of the Central Eskimos. Report of the Fifth Thule Expedition – Vol. 4/1 (Copenhagen 1927).

Mathiassen 1927b: T. Mathiassen, The Thule culture and its position within the Eskimo culture. Archaeology of the Central Eskimos – Vol 2 (Copenhagen 1927).

Mathiassen 1929: T. Mathiassen, The archaeological collection of the Cambridge East Greenland Expedition 1926. Meddelelser om Grønland 74 (Copenhagen 1929) 137–166.

Mathiassen 1930: T. Mathiassen, Inugsuk – a medieval Eskimo settlement in Upernavik district, West Greenland. Meddelelser om Grønland 77 (Copenhagen 1930) 147–340.

Mathiassen 1931: T. Mathiassen, Ancient Eskimo settlements in the Kangâmiut area. Meddelelser om Grønland 91/1 (Copenhagen 1931).

Mathiassen 1934: T. Mathiassen, Contributions to the archaeology of Disko Bay. Meddelelser om Grønland 93/2 (Copenhagen 1934).

Mathiassen 1945: T. Mathiassen, Material culture of the Iglulik Eskimos. Report of the Fifth Thule Expedition – Vol. 6/2 (Copenhagen 1945).

Maxwell 1985: M. S. Maxwell, Prehistory of the Eastern Arctic (Orlando 1985).

McCullough 1989: K. M. McCullough, The Ruin islanders – Early Thule culture pioneers in the Eastern High Arctic (Hull 1989).

McEwen et al. 1991: E. McEwen / R. Miller / C. Bergman, Early bow design and construction. Scientific American 264, 1991, 76–82.

McGhee 1984: R. McGhee, Thule prehistory of Canada. In: D. Damas (Ed.), Handbook of North American Indians – Vol. 5 (Washington 1984) 369–376.

McGhee 2001: R. McGhee, Ancient people of the Arctic (Vancouver 2001).

Meldgaard 1982: J. Meldgaard, Aron – En af de mærkværdigste billedsamlinger i verden (Copenhagen 1982).

Meldgaard 1986: M. Meldgaard, The Greenland caribou – zoogeography, taxonomy, and population dynamics. Meddelelser om Grønland, Bioscience 20 (Odense 1986).

Miller et al. 1986: R. Miller / E. McEwen / C. Bergmann, Experimental approaches to ancient Near Eastern archery. World Archaeology 18, 1986, 178–195.

Möller 1981–83: C. Möller, Das Erweichen von Geweih durch Wasseraufnahme. Hammaburg Neue Forschungen 6, 1981–83, 229–232.

Murdoch 1890: J. Murdoch, A study of the Eskimo bows in the U.S. National Museum. Report of the Smithsonian Institution 1883–84 – Vol. 2 (Washington 1890) 307–316.

Muus et al. 1990: B. Muus / F. Salomonsen / C. Vibe, Grønlands fauna (Copenhagen ²1990).

Nathorst 1900: A. G. Nathorst, Twaa somrar i norra ishafvet – Vol. 2 (Stockholm 1900).

NTNU Vitenskapsmuseet 2008: NTNU Vitenskapsmuseet (Ed.), Døden eller Grønlands vestkyst. Fridtjof Nansens Grønlandsexpedition 1888–89 og Det internationale Polaråret 2007–2008 (Trondheim 2008).

Pasda 2011: C. Pasda, Karibujäger in Grönland – Die Ergebnisse der archäologischen Untersuchungen von 2005–2009 im hinteren Nuuk–Fjord. Internationale Archäologie 116 (Rahden/Westf 2011).

Paulsen 1999: H. Paulsen, Pfeil und Bogen in Haithabu. Berichte Ausgrabungen in Haithabu 33 (Schleswig 1999).

Petersen 1986: H. C. Petersen, Skinboats of Greenland. Ships and boats of the North – Vol. 1 (Roskilde 1986).

Petersen 2003: R. Petersen, Settlement, kinship and hunting grounds in traditional Greenland. Meddelelser om Grønland, Man and Society 27 (Copenhagen 2003).

Pétillon 2013: J.-M. Pétillon, Circulation of whale-bone artifacts in the northern Pyrenees during the Late Upper Paleolithic. Journal of Human Evolution 65, 2013, 525–543.

Pfeifer 2014: S. Pfeifer, Von Grönland zum Petersfels – taphonomische Untersuchungen an rezenten Rentiergeweihen und ihre Relevanz für die Archäologie. Archäologisches Korrespondenzblatt 44/1, 2014, 11–28.

Pfeifer et al. 2019: S. J. Pfeifer / W. L. Hartramph / R.–D. Kahlke / F. A. Müller, Proboscidean ivory was the most suitable osseous raw material for Late Pleistocene big game projectiles. Scientific Reports 2019. https://doi.org/10.1038/s41598–019–38779–1

Pope 1923: S. T. Pope, A study of bows and arrows. University of California Publications in American Archaeology and Ethnology 13, 1923, 329–414.

Porsild 1915a: M. P. Porsild, Studies on the material culture of the Eskimo in West Greenland. Meddelelser om Grønland 51 (Copenhagen 1915) 111–250.

Porsild 1915b: M. P. Porsild, The principle of the screw in the technique of the Eskimo. American Anthropologist 17, 1915, 1–16.

Raghavan et al. 2014: M. Raghavan / M. DeGiorgio / A. Albrechtsen / I. Moltke / P. Skoglund / T. S. Korneliussen / B. Grønnow / M. Appelt / H. C. Gulløv / M. Friesen / W. Fitzhugh / H. Malmström / S. Rasmussen / J. Olsen / L. Melchior / B. T. Fuller / S. M. Fahrni / T. Stafford Jr. / V. Grimes / M. A. Priscilla Renouf / J. Cybulski / N. Lynnerup / M. Mirazon Lahr / K. Britton / R. Knecht / J. Arneborg / M. Metspalu / O. E. Cornejo / A.-S. Malaspinas / Y. Wang / M. Rasmussen / V. Raghavan / T. V. O. Hansen / E. Khusnutdinova / T. Pierre / K. Dneprovsky / C. Andreasen / H. Lange / M. G. Hayes / J. Coltrain / V. A. Spitsyn / A. Götherström / L. Orlando / T. Kivisild / R. Villems / M. H. Crawford / F. C. Nielsen / J. Dissing / J. Heinemeier / M. Meldgaard / C. Bustamante / D. H. O 'Rourke / M. Jakobsson / M.

T. P. Gilbert / R. Nielsen / E. Willerslev, The genetic prehistory of the New World Arctic. Science 345, 2014. www.doi.org/10.1126/science.1255832

Rasmussen 1926: K. Rasmussen, Fra Grønland til Stillehavet. Rejser og mennesker fra 5. Thule Expedition – Vol. 2 (Copenhagen 1926).

Richter 1934: S. Richter, A contribution to the archaeology of North-East Greenland. Skrifter om Svalbard og Ishavet 63 (Oslo 1934).

Riesch 2002: H. Riesch, Pfeil und Bogen zur Merowingerzeit. Eine Quellenkunde und Rekonstruktion des frühmittelalterlichen Bogenschießens (Wald-Michelbach 2002).

Roth 2004: R. Roth, Histoire de l'archerie, arc et arbalète (Paris 2004).

Ryder 1895: C. H. Ryder, Om den tidligere eskimoiske bebyggelse af Scoresby Sund. Meddelelser om Grønland 17 (Copenhagen 1895) 3–21.

Secher et al. 1987: K. Secher / J. Bøcher / B. Grønnow / S. Holt / H. C. Petersen / H. Thing, Arnangarngup Qoorua. Paradisdal i tusinder af år (Nuuk 1987).

Steensby 1910: H. P. Steensby, Contributions to the ethnology and anthropogeography of the Polar Eskimos (Copenhagen 1910).

Sørensen and Gulløv 2012: M. Sørensen and H. C. Gulløv, The prehistory of Inuit in Northeast Greenland. Arctic Anthropology 49, 2012, 88–104.

Stefánsson 1914: V. Stefánsson, The Stefánsson-Anderson Arctic Expedition of the American Museum: Preliminary ethnological report. Anthropological Papers of the American Museum of Natural History 14/1 (New York 1914).

Stodiek 1993: U. Stodiek, Zur Technologie der jungpaläolithischen Speerschleuder – Eine Studie auf der Basis archäologischer, ethnologischer und experimenteller Erkenntnisse. Tübinger Monografien zur Urgeschichte 9 (Tübingen 1993).

Szewciw et al. 2010: L. Szewciw / D. De Kerckhove / G. Grime / D. S. Fudge, Calcification provides mechanical reinforcement to whale baleen α-keratin. Proceedings of the Royal Society of London B: Biological Sciences 277, 2010, 2597–2605.

Taylor 1974: J. G. Taylor, Netsilik Eskimo material culture – The Roald Amundsen Collection from King William Island (Oslo / Bergen / Tromsø 1974).

Thomsen 1917: T. Thomsen, Implements and artefacts of the North-east Greenlanders. Meddelelser om Grønland 44 (Copenhagen 1917) 357–496.

Thomsen 1928: T. Thomsen, Eskimo archaeology. In: M. Vahl / G. C. Amdrup / S. Jensen (Eds), Greenland – Vol. 2 (Copenhagen / London 1928) 271–329.

Tuborg Sandell and Sandell 1991: H. Tuborg Sandell and B. Sandell, Archaeology and environment in the Scoresby Sund fjord – Ethno-archaeological investigations of the last Thule culture of Northeast Greenland. Meddelelser om Grønland, Man and society 15 (Copenhagen 1991).

Tukura 1994: D. Tukura, African archery. In: J. Hamm (Ed.), The traditional bowyer's bible – Vol. 3 (New York 1994) 143–162.

UNESCO 1557: Aasivissuit – Nipisat. Inuit hunting ground between ice and sea. https://whc.unesco.org/en/list/1557/

M. Walls, Paleocarpentry in the Eastern Arctic: an inferential exploration of Saqqaq kayak construction. Explorations in Anthropology 10, 2010, 96–109.

Webster and Zibell 1970: D. H. Webster and W. Zibell, Inupiat Eskimo dictionary (Fairbanks 1970).

Weniger 1987: G.-C. Weniger, Der kantabrische Harpunentyp. Überlegungen zur Morphologie und Klassifikation einer magdalénienzeitlichen Widerhakenspitze. Madrider Mitteilungen 28, 1987, 1–43.

Appendix

A1 – Studied bows of the Greenland Thule culture

Inv.-number	Source of data	Depository	Provenance	Dating	Context	Collector	Year of acquisition	Comment
Polar Greenland								
L. 4334	Steensby 1910	Greenland National Museum	Uummannaq (Thule) (76°33.5′N 68°46.6′W)	1909	ethnographic	no inf.	1909	model
Lu. 323	this study	National Museum of Denmark	Uummannaq (Thule) (76°33.5′N 68°46.6′W)	beginning 20th cent.	ethnographic	Holtved	no inf.	model
L.3.12147	Holtved 1954	National Museum of Denmark	Nuullit (76°48.8′N 70°35.2′W)	13th–14th cent.	settlement	Holtved	1947	model
L 17.111	this study	National Museum of Denmark	Polar Greenland	beginning 20th cent.	ethnographic	Nordmann	1942	model
L. 10300	this study	National Museum of Denmark	Polar Greenland	1900–1970	ethnographic	no inf.	2013	model
Lu. 324	this study	National Museum of Denmark	Uummannaq (Thule) (76°33.5′N 68°46.6′W)	beginning 20th cent.	ethnographic	no inf.	no inf.	model
Lu. 325	Steensby 1910	Greenland National Museum	Uummannaq (Thule) (76°33.5′N 68°46.6′W)	beginning 20th cent.	ethnographic	no inf.	no inf.	model
x. 173	Steensby 1910	Greenland National Museum	Polar Greenland	beginning 20th cent.	ethnographic	Steensby	no inf.	model
x. 174	this study	National Museum of Denmark	Polar Greenland	beginning 20th cent.	ethnographic	Steensby	no inf.	model
L 17.88	this study	National Museum of Denmark	Polar Greenland and Ellesmere Island	no inf.	no inf.	Nielsen	1938	found and repaired by Polar Inuit
Northwest Greenland								
A.2.c.4	this study	National Museum of Denmark	Uummannaq Ø (70°40.3′N 52°07.4′W)	no inf.	grave	no inf.	no inf.	
L. 4568	this study	National Museum of Denmark	Disko (69°48′N 53°21′W)	no inf.	grave	Porsild	no inf.	
L. 4569	this study	National Museum of Denmark	Disko (69°48′N 53°21′W)	no inf.	grave	Porsild	no inf.	
L. 1957	Birket-Smith 1918	Greenland National Museum	Nuussuaq - Akunak (70°25.0′N 52°30.0′W)	no inf.	grave	no inf.	no inf.	belongs to arrow L. 1958.2 see Fig. 2.6
L. 2881	this study	National Museum of Denmark	Disko (69°48′N 53°21′W)	no inf.	no inf.	no inf.	no inf.	
L. 5658	this study	National Museum of Denmark	Upernivik (71°16′N 52°45′W)	no inf.	no inf.	no inf.	no inf.	

Inv.-number	Source of data	Depository	Provenance	Dating	Context	Collector	Year of acquisition	Comment
L. 7861	this study	National Museum of Denmark	Uummannaq Ø (70°40.3'N 52°07.4'W)	no inf.	no inf.	no inf.	no inf.	
L. 8857	Birket-Smith 1918	Greenland National Museum	Uummannaq Ø (70°40.3'N 52°07.4'W)	no inf.	no inf.	no inf.	no inf.	
Lc. 293	museum records	Greenland National Museum	Uummannaq Ø (70°40.3'N 52°07.4'W)	no inf.	grave	Friis	1849	
Lc. 356	this study	National Museum of Denmark	Northwest Greenland	no inf.	grave	Fleischer	1851	
West Greenland								
Lc. 81	this study	National Museum of Denmark	Southwest Greenland?	no inf.	grave	Holbøll	1840	
Lc. 365	Birket-Smith 1918	Greenland National Museum	West Greenland	no inf.	grave	Sommer	1853	see Fig. 2.6
Lu. 709	Museum records	Greenland National Museum	West Greenland	no inf.	no inf.	no inf.	no inf.	
Central West Greenland								
L. 6.685	this study	National Museum of Denmark	Illutalik (Ilulissat district)	15th cent.	settlement	Mathiassen	1933	
L. 6.781	this study	National Museum of Denmark	Illutalik (Ilulissat district)	15th cent.	settlement	Mathiassen	1933	
L. 6.884	this study	National Museum of Denmark	Illutalik (Ilulissat district)	15th cent.	settlement	Mathiassen	1933	
L. 6.3719	Mathiassen 1934	Greenland National Museum	Qeqertaq (69°59.5'N 51°18.1'W)	no inf.	settlement	Mathiassen	1933	
L 12.1952	this study	National Museum of Denmark	Qeqertarmiut (Maniitsoq district)	1350–1500	settlement	Mathiassen	1930	
L. 4386	Birket-Smith 1918	Greenland National Museum	Ilulissat (69°12.6'N 51°6.0'W)	no inf.	no inf.	no inf.	no inf.	
L. 4817	Birket-Smith 1918	Greenland National Museum	Kangerluarsuk (65°25.1'N 52°31.4'W)	no inf.	no inf.	no inf.	no inf.	
L. 5966	this study	National Museum of Denmark	Sermermiut (69°12.7'N 51°7.3'W)	no inf.	no inf.	Mathiassen	1958	
L. 8565	Birket-Smith 1918	Greenland National Museum	Kangaamiut (65°49.0'N 53°19.0'W)	no inf.	no inf.	no inf.	no inf.	
Lb. 1	this study	National Museum of Denmark	Nuuk Fjord	17th cent.	no inf.	Kunstkammer	end of 17th cent.	
Lb. 35	this study	National Museum of Denmark	Aasiaat (68°42.4'N 52°52.1'W)	no inf.	grave	Rudolph	1856	
Lb. 134	Birket-Smith 1918	Greenland National Museum	Sermermiut (69°12.7'N 51°7.3'W)	no inf.	grave	Krarup-Smith	1873	

Inv.-number	Source of data	Depository	Provenance	Dating	Context	Collector	Year of acquisition	Comment
Lb. 190	this study	National Museum of Denmark	Aasiaat (68°42.4'N 52°52.1'W) - Aito	no inf.	grave	no inf.	1874	
Lb. 194	this study	National Museum of Denmark	Qasigiannguit - Qeqertasussuk (68°49.1'N 51°11.4'W)	no inf.	grave	Krarup-Smith	1874	
Lb. 232	this study	National Museum of Denmark	Qasigiannguit - Qeqertasussuk (68°49.1'N 51°11.4'W)	no inf.	grave	Krarup-Smith	1876	
Lb. 233	this study	National Museum of Denmark	Qasigiannguit - Qeqertasussuk (68°49.1'N 51°11.4'W)	no inf.	grave	Krarup-Smith	1876	
Trondheim bow	NTNU Vitenskabsmuseet 2008	Vitenskabsmuseet Trondheim	Nuuk Fjord	18th cent.	ethnographic	no inf.	18th cent.	
Bergen painting	this study	National Museum of Denmark	Nuuk Fjord	1654	ethnographic	no inf.	no inf.	
Copenhagen painting	this study	National Museum of Denmark	Nuuk Fjord	1724	ethnographic	Grodtschilling	no inf.	Qiperoq and Pooq
Northeast Greenland								
Bartlett bows	Bartlett 1931	National Museum of the American Indian	Shannon Ø (75°08.0'N 18°25.0'W)	pre-19th cent.	settlement	Bartlett Exp.	1930	2 bows, from house ruin
Cambridge Expedition	Mathiassen 1929	MAA Cambridge	Eleonore Bugt (73°26.6'N 25°22.8'W)	pre-19th cent.	stray find	Cambridge Exp.	1926	2 bows
No. 2582	Larsen 1934	Greenland National Museum	Dødemandsbugten (74°06.8'N 20°53.6'W)	15th–16th cent.	settlement	Larsen	1934	
Grave 6	Larsen 1934	Greenland National Museum	Dødemandsbugten (74°06.8'N 20°53.6'W)	15th–16th cent.	grave	Larsen	1934	
KNK 566	Tuborg Sandell and Sandell 1991	Greenland National Museum	Kap Stewart (70°27'N 22°38'W)	beginning of 19th cent.	settlement	Sandell/ Tuborg Sandell	1991	
L 1.3527	this study	National Museum of Denmark	Geographical Society Ø (72°57.0'N 23°30.0'W)	no inf.	settlement	Glob	1933	from house ruin
L 1.3867	this study	National Museum of Denmark	Kempe Fjord (72°48.0'N 25°50.0'W)	no inf.	settlement	Glob	1933	from house ruin
L 1.4183	this study	National Museum of Denmark	Kempe Fjord (72°48.0'N 25°50.0'W)	no inf.	settlement	Glob	1933	from house ruin
L 1.4293	this study	National Museum of Denmark	Suess Land (72°59.0'N 26°20.0'W)	no inf.	grave	Glob	1933	see Fig. 3.3

Inv.-number	Source of data	Depository	Provenance	Dating	Context	Collector	Year of acquisition	Comment
L 1.4401	this study	National Museum of Denmark	no inf. „Kap Hedelund‘	no inf.	stray find	no inf.	no inf.	
L 1.522	Ryder 1895	Greenland National Museum	Kap Hope (70°27.3'N 22°19.5'W)	beginning of 19th cent.	grave	Danish East Greenland Exp.	no inf.	
L. 3244	Thomsen 1917	Greenland National Museum	17 kilometernæsset (76°49.3'N 18°17.2'W)	no inf.	settlement	Danmark Exp.	1908	from tent ring
L. 3327	this study	National Museum of Denmark	Maroussia (76°39.5'N 18°30.6'W)	no inf.	settlement	Danmark Exp.	1908	from house ruin
L. 3660	this study	National Museum of Denmark	Stormbugtens Østkyst (76°46'N 19°00'W)	no inf.	settlement	Danmark Exp.	1908	from house ruin
L. 3661	this study	National Museum of Denmark	Stormbugtens Østkyst (76°46'N 19°00'W)	no inf.	settlement	Danmark Exp.	1908	from house ruin
L. 3862	this study	National Museum of Denmark	Snenæs (76°49.2'N 19°21.4'W)	no inf.	settlement	Danmark Exp.	1908	from house ruin
L. 4058	this study	National Museum of Denmark	Rypefjeldet (76°56.2'N 20°22.1'W)	no inf.	settlement	Danmark Exp.	1908	from house ruin
L. 4059	this study	National Museum of Denmark	Rypefjeldet (76°56.2'N 20°22.1'W)	no inf.	settlement	Danmark Exp.	1908	from house ruin
Lc. 1424	this study	National Museum of Denmark	Danmark Ø (70°30'N 26°15'W)	no inf.	stray find	Danish East Greenland Exp.	1892	
Nathorst bow	Nathorst 1900	no inf.	Kap Weber (73°30.0'N 24°43.3'W)	pre-19th cent.	stray find	Nathorst Exp.	1899	
Norwegian hunter's find	Richter 1934	Greenland National Museum	Gauss Halvø (73°30.0'N 23°00.0'W)	pre-19th cent.	stray find	no inf.	no inf.	see Fig. 3.2
Richter bows	Richter 1934	Greenland National Museum	Gauss Halvø (73°30.0'N 23°00.0'W)	pre-19th cent.	settlement	Richter campaign	no inf.	4 bows
Schwach's find	this study	National Museum of Denmark	Hochstetter Forland (75°25.0'N 19°48.0'W)	no inf.	stray find	no inf.	no inf.	
Southeast Greenland								
L. 6615	Amdrup 1902	Greenland National Museum	north of Ammassalik „Depotøen‘	no inf.	settlement	Carlsberg Exp.	1898–1900	from house ruin
L. 6617	this study	National Museum of Denmark	north of Ammassalik „Depotøen‘	no inf.	stray find	Carlsberg Exp.	1898–1900	

A2 – Studied arrows of the Greenland Thule culture

Inv.-number	Source of data	Depository	Provenance	Dating	Context	Collector	Year of acquisition	Comment
Polar Greenland								
Lu. 323	this study	National Museum of Denmark	Uummannaq (Thule) (76°33.5'N 68°46.6'W)	early 20th cent.	ethnographic	Holtved	beginning 20th cent.	4 arrows, set with bow Lu. 323
Lu. 324	this study	National Museum of Denmark	Polar Greenland	early 20th cent.	ethnographic	no inf.	beginning 20th cent.	2 arrows, models
Lu. 327	this study	National Museum of Denmark	Uummannaq (Thule) (76°33.5'N 68°46.6'W)	early 20th cent.	ethnographic	no inf.	beginning 20th cent.	2 arrows, models
x. 173	this study	National Museum of Denmark	Polar Greenland	early 20th cent.	ethnographic	Steensby	1921	4 arrows, models
L 17.89	this study	National Museum of Denmark	Polar Greenland, Ellesmere Island	no inf.	grave and ethnographic	Nielsen	1938	18 arrows, found with bow L 17.88
Northwest Greenland								
L. 1958.2	this study	National Museum of Denmark	Nuussuaq Peninsula (70°25.0'N 52°30.0'W)	no inf.	grave	no inf.	no inf.	found with bow L. 1957
West Greenland								
L 17.112	this study	National Museum of Denmark	West Greenland	no inf.	grave	Nordmann	1942	
L. 2880	this study	National Museum of Denmark	West Greenland	no inf.	no inf.	no inf.	no inf.	5 arrows
Lb. 3	this study	National Museum of Denmark	West Greenland	no inf.	grave	Rudolph	1854	
Lb. 4	museum records	Greenland National Museum	West Greenland	no inf.	grave	Rudolph	1854	
Lb. 111	this study	National Museum of Denmark	West Greenland	no inf.	no inf.	Oldskriftsselskab	1867	3 arrows
Lb. 116	this study	National Museum of Denmark	West Greenland	no inf.	grave	Olrik	1868	2 arrows
Lb. 117	museum records	Greenland National Museum	West Greenland	no inf.	stray find	Olrik	1868	
Lb. 579	this study	National Museum of Denmark	West Greenland	no inf.	grave	Ryberg	1889	from Samuel Kleinschmidt
Lc. 343	museum records	Greenland National Museum	West Greenland	no inf.	grave	Olrik	1851	

Inv.-number	Source of data	Depository	Provenance	Dating	Context	Collector	Year of acquisition	Comment
Lu. 705	this study	National Museum of Denmark	West Greenland	no inf.	no inf.	no inf.	no inf.	2 arrows
Central West Greenland								
L. 6.885	this study	National Museum of Denmark	Illutalik (Ilulissat district)	15th cent.	settlement	Mathiassen	1933	
L. 8.1789	this study	National Museum of Denmark	Sermermiut (69°12.7'N 51°7.3'W)	starting with 14th cent.	settlement	Mathiassen	1955	
L. 8.1839	this study	National Museum of Denmark	Sermermiut (69°12.7'N 51°7.3'W)	starting with 14th cent.	settlement	Mathiassen	1955	
L. 8.1953	this study	National Museum of Denmark	Sermermiut (69°12.7'N 51°7.3'W)	starting with 14th cent.	settlement	Mathiassen	1955	
L. 8.1954	this study	National Museum of Denmark	Sermermiut (69°12.7'N 51°7.3'W)	starting with 14th cent.	settlement	Mathiassen	1955	
L. 8.1955	this study	National Museum of Denmark	Sermermiut (69°12.7'N 51°7.3'W)	starting with 14th cent.	settlement	Mathiassen	1955	
L. 8.1956	this study	National Museum of Denmark	Sermermiut (69°12.7'N 51°7.3'W)	starting with 14th cent.	settlement	Mathiassen	1955	
L. 1661	this study	National Museum of Denmark	Ilulissat (69°12.6'N 51°6.0'W)	no inf.	grave	no inf.	no inf.	
L. 2878	this study	National Museum of Denmark	Central West Greenland	no inf.	grave	no inf.	no inf.	5 arrows
L. 2879	this study	National Museum of Denmark	Central West Greenland	no inf.	grave	no inf.	no inf.	2 arrows
L. 5965	this study	National Museum of Denmark	Sermermiut (69°12.7'N 51°7.3'W)	starting with 14th cent.	settlement	Mathiassen	1955	
Lb. 80	museum records	Greenland National Museum	Aasiaat - Aito (68°42.4'N 52°52.1'W)	no inf.	grave	Pfaff	1863	
Lb. 81	museum records	Greenland National Museum	Aasiaat - Aito (68°42.4'N 52°52.1'W)	no inf.	grave	Pfaff	1863	
Lb. 84	this study	National Museum of Denmark	Aasiaat - Aito (68°42.4'N 52°52.1'W)	no inf.	grave	Pfaff	1863	found with bow
Lb. 195	museum records	Greenland National Museum	Ilulissat (69°12.6'N 51°6.0'W) , Qeqertasussuk'	no inf.	stray find	Krarup-Smidt	1867	

Inv.-number	Source of data	Depository	Provenance	Dating	Context	Year of acquisition	Collector	Comment
Lb. 201	museum records	Greenland National Museum	Aasiaat - Niarkorniasuk (68°42.4'N 52°52.1'W)	no inf.	no inf.	1867	Krarup-Smidt	
Lb. 216	museum records	Greenland National Museum	‘Eginiartik‘ Iginniarfik(?) (68°08.5'N 53°10.2'W)	no inf.	no inf.	1876	Krarup-Smidt	
Lb. 219	museum records	Greenland National Museum	Aasiaat - Niarkorniasuk (68°42.4'N 52°52.1'W)	no inf.	no inf.	1867	Krarup-Smidt	
Lb. 430	this study	National Museum of Denmark	Central West Greenland	no inf.	grave	1887	Horring	4 arrows
Lc. 32b	this study	National Museum of Denmark	Nuuk Fjord	17th cent.	ethnographic	1674	Kunstkammer	
Lu. 704	this study	National Museum of Denmark	Ilulissat (69°12.6'N 51°6.0'W)	no inf.	grave	1933	Mathiassen	
"Sukkertoppen Distr"	this study	National Museum of Denmark	Maniitsoq district	no inf.	no inf.	no inf.	no inf.	
Bergen Painting	this study	National Museum of Denmark	Nuuk Fjord	1654	ethnographic	no inf.	Kunstkammer	
Copenhagen Painting	this study	National Museum of Denmark	Nuuk Fjord	1724	ethnographic	no inf.	Kunstkammer	Qiperoq and Pooq
Northeast Greenland								
KNK 566	Tuborg Sandell and Sandell 1991	Greenland National Museum	Kap Stewart (70°27'N 22°38'W)	beginning of 19th cent.	settlement	1991	excavation KNK	from house ruin
Grave 6	Larsen 1934	Greenland National Museum	Dodemandsbugten (74°06.8'N 20°53.6'W)	15th–16th cent.	grave	1934	Larsen	2 shafts, several points
L 1.6657	this study	National Museum of Denmark	Snenæs (76°49.2'N 19°21.4'W)	no inf.	stray find	1950	Knuth	2 arrows, found together with bow
L. 3048	museum records	Greenland National Museum	Renskæret (76°40.9'N 18°30.9'W)	no inf.	grave	1908	Danmark Exp.	
L. 3663	this study	National Museum of Denmark	Stormbugt (76°46'N 19°00'W)	no inf.	stray find	1908	Danmark Exp.	
L. 3863	museum records	Greenland National Museum	Snenæs (76°49.2'N 19°21.4'W)	no inf.	stray find	1908	Danmark Exp.	

A3 – Bow raw materials

Inv.-number	Stave	Wrappings	Cable backing	Bracers	Growth ring orientation	Growth rings per cm	String	Comment
A.2.c.4	baleen	no inf.	no inf.	-	-	-	no inf.	
L 1.3527	no inf.	no inf.	no inf.	no inf.	diagonal	18	no inf.	
L 1.3867	no inf.	no inf.	no inf.	no inf.	horizontal	20	no inf.	
L 1.4183	no inf.	no inf.	no inf.	no inf.	no inf.	no inf.	no inf.	
L 1.4293	wood	no inf.	no inf.	no inf.	vertical	6	no inf.	smooth surface
L 1.4401	wood	no inf.	no inf.	no inf.	diagonal	18	no inf.	
L 6.685	wood	no inf.	no inf.	no inf.	horizontal	no inf.	no inf.	
L 6.781	baleen	no inf.	no inf.	-	-	-	no inf.	
L 6.884	wood	no inf.	no inf.	no inf	horizontal	no inf.	no inf.	smooth surface
L 12.1952	wood	no inf.	no inf.	no inf.	horizontal	no inf.	no inf.	smooth surface
L 17.111	antler	rawhide	rawhide	antler, tusk	-	-	rawhide	smooth surface
L. 2881	wood	no inf.	no inf.	-	diagonal	5	no inf.	smooth surface
L. 3327	baleen	no inf.	no inf.	-	-	-	no inf.	
L. 3660	wood	no inf.	no inf.	no inf.	horizontal	8	no inf.	
L. 3661	wood	no inf.	no inf.	no inf.	vertical	4	no inf.	
L. 3862	wood	no inf.	no inf.	no inf.	no inf.	no inf.	no inf.	overgrown with lichen
L. 4058	wood	no inf.	no inf.	no inf.	vertical	8	no inf.	
L. 4059	wood	no inf.	no inf.	no inf.	vertical	no inf.	no inf.	
L. 4568	wood	no inf.	no inf.	no inf.	horizontal	5	no inf.	
L. 4569	wood	no inf.	no inf.	no inf.	horizontal	8	no inf.	
L. 5658	baleen	no inf.	no inf.	-	-	-	no inf.	
L. 5966	wood	no inf.	no inf.	no inf.	horizontal	no inf.	no inf.	
L. 6617	wood	no inf.	no inf.	no inf.	horizontal	no inf.	no inf.	
L. 7861	baleen	no inf.	no inf.	-	-	-	no inf.	smooth surface
L. 10300	antler	rawhide	sinew	antler	-	-	sinew	smooth surface
Lb. 1	wood, baleen	rawhide, sinew	rawhide, sinew	antler	horizontal, diagonal	9	no inf.	shiny surface, polished
Lb. 35	wood	no inf.	no inf.	-	diagonal	4	no inf.	shiny surface, polished
Lb. 190	wood	no inf.	no inf.	-	diagonal	10	no inf.	
Lb. 194	wood	no inf.	sinew	-	horizontal	12	no inf.	many small branches
Lb. 232	wood	no inf.	no inf.	-	horizontal	5	no inf.	shiny surface, polished

Inv.-number	Stave	Wrappings	Cable backing	Bracers	Growth ring orientation	Growth rings per cm	String	Comment
Lb. 233	wood	no inf.	no inf.	-	horizontal	12	no inf.	shiny surface, polished
Lc. 81	wood	no inf.	no inf.	-	horizontal	15	no inf.	shiny surface, polished
Lc. 356	baleen	no inf.	no inf.	-	-	-	no inf.	smooth surface
Lc. 1424	wood	no inf.	no inf.	no inf.	horizontal	6	no inf.	smooth surface
Lu. 323	antler	sinew	sinew	antler	-	-	sinew	smooth surface
Lu. 324	antler	sinew	sinew	antler	-	-	sinew	smooth surface
Schwach's find	wood	no inf.	no inf.	no inf.	diagonal	9	no inf.	smooth surface
x. 174	antler	sinew	sinew	antler	-	-	sinew	
Bergen painting	wood	no inf.	no inf.	-	no inf.	no inf.	no inf.	
Copenhagen painting	wood	no inf.	no inf.	-	no inf.	no inf.	no inf.	

A4 – Bow measurements (in cm)

Measurements printed **bold** are incomplete.

Inv.-number	Total length	Width handle	Width upper limb	Width lower limb	Width upper tip	Width lower tip	Thick-ness handle	Thickness upper limb	Thickness lower limb	Thickness upper tip	Thickness lower tip	Comment
A.2.c.4	**96 (104 rec.)**	2.9	3.3	3.3	no inf.	3.3	1.7	1.8	1.8	no inf.	**0.9**	lower tip decayed
L 1.3527	**28.6**	no inf.	3.6	no inf.	**2.8**	no inf.	no inf.	1.4	no inf.	1.9	no inf.	decayed
L 1.3867	**12.5**	no inf.	no inf.	no inf.	3.6	no inf.	no inf.	no inf.	no inf.	1.7	no inf.	only tip
L 1.4183	**30**	no inf.	**3.8**	no inf.	**3.5**	no inf.	no inf.	no inf.	no inf.	**1.5**	no inf.	decayed
L 1.4293	106.8	2.3	3.4	3.5	2.5	2.4	1.7	1	1.1	1.5	1.4	lower tip decayed
L 1.4401	**51**	no inf.	3.7	no inf.	3.9	no inf.	no inf.	1.2	no inf.	1.9	no inf.	only rear end
L 6.685	**15.3**	no inf.	no inf.	no inf.	**2.5 (3 rec.)**	no inf.	no inf.	no inf.	no inf.	1.6	no inf.	only tip
L 6.781	**9.7**	no inf.	no inf.	no inf.	**1.9**	no inf.	no inf.	no inf.	no inf.	1	no inf.	only tip
L 6.884	**10.1**	no inf.	no inf.	no inf.	3	no inf.	no inf.	no inf.	no inf.	1.4	no inf.	only tip
L 12.1952	**8.9**	no inf.	no inf.	no inf.	2.3	no inf.	no inf.	no inf.	no inf.	1.1	no inf.	only tip
L 17.111	70.3	2.8	2.6	2.7	2.9	3.1	1.3	0.9	1.1	0.9	0.8	
L 2881	97.6	2.9	3.3	3	**2.5**	2.9	1.7	1.4	1.5	1.2	1.1	
L. 3327	**12.1**	no inf.	no inf.	no inf.	2.4	no inf.	no inf.	no inf.	no inf.	no inf.	no inf.	only tip
L.3660	77	2.2	2.8	2.6	no inf.	no inf.	1.8	1.2	1.4	no inf.	no inf.	only handle section

Inv-number	Total length	Width handle	Width upper limb	Width lower limb	Width upper tip	Width lower tip	Thick-ness handle	Thickness upper limb	Thickness lower limb	Thickness upper tip	Thickness lower tip	Comment
L. 3661	30.8	no inf.	3.4	no inf.	no inf.	no inf.	no inf.	1.4	no inf.	no inf.	no inf.	position unclear
L. 3862	78.1	2.4	3.4	3.3	no inf.	no inf.	2	1.4	1.4	no inf.	no inf.	only handle section
L. 4058	19.4	no inf.	no inf.	no inf.	2.8	no inf.	no inf.	no inf.	no inf.	1.2	no inf.	only tip
L. 4059	38.3	2.8	no inf.	no inf.	no inf.	no inf.	2.9	no inf.	no inf.	no inf.	no inf.	position unclear
L. 4568	118	2.6	3.4	3.4	2.7	2.7	1.8	1.6	1.5	1.4	1.4	rear ends broken
L. 4569	62.9	2.8	3.5	3.4	no inf.	no inf.	1.8	1.3	1.3	no inf.	no inf.	only handle section
L. 5658	58.5	no inf.	3.2	no inf.	3.1	no inf.	no inf.	0.8	no inf.	1.1	no inf.	one layer
L. 5966	20.7	no inf.	no inf.	no inf.	2.1	no inf.	no inf.	1.7	no inf.	1.3	no inf.	decayed
L. 6617	32.7	no inf.	3.4	no inf.	no inf.	no inf.	no inf.	1.7	no inf.	no inf.	no inf.	position unclear
L. 7861	82.1	1.7	2.5	2.4	1.9	2.3	1.3	1.4	1.3	0.7	0.7	upper tip decayed
L. 10300	74.4	2.7	2.4	2.5	2.1	2.2	1.1	0.5	0.5	0.4	0.4	
Lb. 1	135 (136 rec.)	2.9	3.5	3.7	3.2	no inf.	2.3	1.5	1.6	1.4	no inf.	lower tip decayed
Lb. 35	158	3.2	3.7	3.8	3.3	3.2	2.7	2.3	2.3	1.8	1.8	
Lb. 190	116.5	2.7	no inf.	3.3	no inf.	no inf.	2	no inf.	1.5	no inf.	no inf.	decayed, worm holes
Lb. 194	134.4	2.8	3.3	3.2	2.9	3.1	2.1	1.7	1.6	1.3	1.3	
Lb. 232	128.4	2.8	3.5	3.4	2.6	2.4	1.9	1.3	1.3	1.3	1.4	
Lb. 233	144	2.7	3.4	3.4	3.3	no inf.	2.3	1.9	1.7	2	no inf.	lower tip decayed
Lc. 81	147.5	3.3	4.2	4.3	2.7	3	2.3	1.8	1.8	1.5	1.7	upper tip decayed
Lc. 356	118.3	2.9	3.2	3.3	2.8	2.7	1.8	1.7	1.7	1	1	lower tip decayed
Lc. 1424	92.5 (150 rec.)	2.7	3.9	no inf.	2.9	no inf.	1.8	1.5	no inf.	2.2	no inf.	lower limb decayed
Lu. 323	79.5	2.8	2.8	2.8	3.2	3.4	1.1	0.7	0.5	0.7	0.8	
Lu. 324	75.3	2.5	2.6	2.4	2.4	2.3	1.2	0.6	0.5	0.5	0.5	
Schwach's find	44.9	no inf.	3.6	no inf.	4	no inf.	no inf.	1.5	no inf.	2.3	no inf.	only rear end
x. 174	89.2	2.5	2.4	2.3	2.8	2.5	1.3	0.6	0.5	0.6	0.5	
Bergen painting	ca. waist high	no inf.	no inf.	no inf.	no inf.	no inf.	no inf.	no inf.	no inf.	no inf.	no inf.	
Copenhagen painting	shoulder high	no inf.	no inf.	no inf.	no inf.	no inf.	no inf.	no inf.	no inf.	no inf.	no inf.	

A5 – Bow design

Inv.-number	Profile	Silhouette	Cross section handle	Cross section mid-limb	Cross section tips
A.2.c.4	triple-curved	straight sides	rectangular	rectangular	rectangular
L 1.3527	triple-curved	no inf.	no inf.	no inf.	rectangular
L 1.3867	no inf.	no inf.	no inf.	no inf.	rectangular
L 1.4183	no inf.	no inf.	no inf.	no inf.	no inf.
L 1.4293	triple-curved	paddle shaped, widened tips	d-shaped	rectangular	d-shaped
L 1.4401	triple-curved	straight sides	no inf.	rectangular	rectangular
L 6.685	no inf.	no inf.	no inf.	no inf.	rectangular
L 6.781	no inf.	no inf.	no inf.	no inf.	no inf.
L 6.884	no inf.	no inf.	no inf.	no inf.	d-shaped
L 12.1952	no inf.	no inf.	no inf.	no inf.	rectangular
L 17.111	double-curved	straight sides, widened tips	d-shaped	d-shaped	d-shaped
L. 2881	d-bow	straight sides, narrowed handle	d-shaped	d-shaped	d-shaped
L. 3327	no inf.	no inf.	no inf.	no inf.	no inf.
L. 3660	triple-curved	no inf.	d-shaped	rectangular	no inf.
L. 3661	no inf.	no inf.	rectangular	no inf.	no inf.
L. 3862	triple-curved	no inf.	d-shaped	rectangular	rectangular
L. 4058	no inf.	no inf.	no inf.	no inf.	no inf.
L. 4059	no inf.	no inf.	no inf.	no inf.	no inf.
L. 4568	triple-curved	paddle shaped, contractions at mid-limb	d-shaped	rectangular	rectangular
L. 4569	triple-curved	no inf.	d-shaped	rectangular	no inf.
L. 5658	recurved	straight sides	no inf.	rectangular	rectangular
L. 5966	d-bow	paddle shaped, widened tips	no inf.	d-shaped	no inf.
L. 6617	d-bow	paddle shaped	rectangular	rectangular	no inf.
L. 7861	triple-curved	paddle shaped, widened tips	rectangular	rectangular	rectangular
L. 10300	double-curved	straight sides	d-shaped	d-shaped	d-shaped
Lb. 1	triple-curved	paddle shaped, widened tips	rectangular	rectangular	no inf.
Lb. 35	d-bow	paddle shaped, widened tips	d-shaped	d-shaped	d-shaped
Lb. 190	d-bow	paddle shaped	rectangular	rectangular	no inf.
Lb. 194	d-bow	straight sides, narrowed handle	d-shaped	d-shaped	d-shaped
Lb. 232	d-bow	paddle shaped	d-shaped	d-shaped	d-shaped
Lb. 233	d-bow	paddle shaped, widened tips	d-shaped	d-shaped	d-shaped

Inv.-number	Profile	Silhouette	Cross section handle	Cross section mid-limb	Cross section tips
Lc. 81	d-bow	paddle shaped, widened tips	d-shaped	triangular	d-shaped
Lc. 356	triple-curved	paddle shaped, widened tips	rectangular	rectangular	rectangular
Lc. 1424	triple-curved	contractions at mid-limb, narrowed handle	d-shaped	rectangular	no inf.
Lu. 323	double-curved	straight sides, widened tips	d-shaped	d-shaped, rectangular	d-shaped, rectangular
Lu. 324	double-curved	straight sides	rectangular	rectangular	rectangular
Schwach's find	triple-curved	straight sides	no inf.	rectangular	rectangular
x. 174	double-curved	straight sides	d-shaped	rectangular	rectangular
Bergen painting	d-bow	no inf.	rectangular	rectangular	rectangular
Copenhagen painting	d-bow	no inf.	no inf.	no inf.	no inf.

A6 – Bow technology

Inv.-number	Bow stave	Cable backing	Number of backing strands	Splices	Comment
A.2.c.4	laminated composite	no inf.	no inf.	-	
L 1.3527	composite	no inf.	no inf.	v-scarf	
L 1.3867	composite	no inf.	no inf.	v-scarf	
L 1.4183	composite	no inf.	no inf.	v-scarf	
L 1.4293	composite	no inf.	no inf.	v-scarf	
L 1.4401	no inf.	no inf.	no inf.	no inf.	
L 6.685	no inf.	no inf.	no inf.	no inf.	reworked piece
L 6.781	laminated composite	no inf.	no inf.	-	
L 6.884	no inf.	no inf.	no inf.	no inf.	
L 12.1952	no inf.	no inf.	no inf.	no inf.	
L 17.111	spliced composite	Eastern	6	splint	backing not twisted
L. 2881	self bow	Arctic	no inf.	-	traces of cable backing at shoulders
L. 3327	laminated composite	no inf.	no inf.	-	
L. 3660	spliced composite	no inf.	no inf.	v-scarf	
L. 3661	spliced composite	no inf.	no inf.	v-scarf	
L. 3862	spliced composite	no inf.	no inf.	v-scarf	
L. 4058	no inf.	no inf.	no inf.	no inf.	
L. 4059	no inf.	no inf.	no inf.	no inf.	
L. 4568	self bow	no inf.	no inf.	-	traces of wrappings

Inv.-number	Bow stave	Cable backing	Number of backing strands	Splices	Comment
L. 4569	spliced composite	no inf.	no inf.	v-scarf	
L. 5658	laminated composite	no inf.	no inf.	-	
L. 5966	no inf.	no inf.	no inf.	no inf.	
L. 6617	spliced composite	no inf.	no inf.	v-scarf	
L. 7861	laminated composite	no inf.	no inf.	-	
L. 10300	spliced composite	Eastern	7	splint	backing not twisted
Lb. 1	laminated composite	Arctic	ca. 30	-	
Lb. 35	self bow	Arctic	no inf.	-	
Lb. 190	self bow	Arctic	no inf.	-	traces of wrapping at handle and shoulders
Lb. 194	self bow	Arctic	no inf.	-	rest of wrapping at upper shoulder
Lb. 232	self bow	Arctic	no inf.	-	
Lb. 233	self bow	Arctic	no inf.	-	
Lc. 81	self bow	Arctic	no inf.	-	
Lc. 356	laminated composite	no inf.	no inf.	-	
Lc. 1424	laminated composite	no inf.	no inf.	-	
Lu. 323	spliced composite	Eastern	13	splint	backing not twisted
Lu. 324	spliced composite	Eastern	7	splint	backing not twisted
Schwach's find	spliced composite	no inf.	no inf.	no inf.	
x. 174	spliced composite	Eastern	6	splint	backing not twisted
Bergen painting	laminated composite	Arctic	no inf.	no inf.	
Copenhagen painting	no inf.	Arctic	no inf.	no inf.	

A7 – Arrow raw materials

Inv.-number	Shaft	Foreshaft	Point	Wrapping tang	Wrapping nock	Wrapping fletching	Feathers	Comment
L. 1.6657	wood	no inf.	no inf.	no inf.	sinew	sinew	tail feathers	
L. 6.885	wood	no inf.	no inf.	no inf.	no inf.	no inf.	no inf.	
L. 8.1789	wood	no inf.	no inf.	no inf.	no inf.	no inf.	no inf.	
L. 8.1839	wood	no inf.	no inf.	no inf.	no inf.	no inf.	no inf.	
L. 8.1953	wood	no inf.	no inf.	no inf.	no inf.	no inf.	no inf.	
L. 8.1954	wood	no inf.	no inf.	no inf.	no inf.	no inf.	no inf.	
L. 8.1955	wood	no inf.	no inf.	no inf.	no inf.	no inf.	no inf.	
L. 8.1956	wood	no inf.	no inf.	no inf.	no inf.	no inf.	no inf.	
L. 17.112	wood	antler	iron	plant fiber	sinew	no inf.	no inf.	
L. 1661	wood	no inf.	no inf.	no inf.	no inf.	no inf.	no inf.	
L. 1958.2	wood	antler	iron	sinew	sinew	sinew	no inf.	
L. 2878a	wood	no inf.	no inf.	no inf.	sinew	sinew	no inf.	fletching glued?
L. 2878b	wood	no inf.	no inf.	no inf.	sinew	sinew	no inf.	fletching glued?
L. 2878c	wood	no inf.	no inf.	no inf.	sinew	sinew	no inf.	fletching glued?
L. 2878d	wood	no inf.	no inf.	no inf.	sinew	sinew	no inf.	fletching glued?
L. 2878e	wood	no inf.	no inf.	no inf.	sinew	sinew	brown feathers	fletching glued?
L. 2879a	wood	no inf.	no inf.	no inf.	no inf.	no inf.	no inf.	
L. 2879b	wood	no inf.	no inf.	no inf.	no inf.	no inf.	no inf.	
L. 2880a	wood	no inf.	no inf.	no inf.	no inf.	no inf.	no inf.	
L. 2880b	wood	no inf.	no inf.	no inf.	no inf.	no inf.	no inf.	
L. 2880c	wood	no inf.	no inf.	no inf.	no inf.	no inf.	no inf.	
L. 2880d	wood	no inf.	no inf.	no inf.	no inf.	no inf.	no inf.	
L. 2880e	wood	no inf.	no inf.	no inf.	no inf.	no inf.	no inf.	
L. 3663	wood	no inf.	no inf.	no inf.	no inf.	no inf.	no inf.	
L.b. 3	wood	-	antler	no inf.	sinew	sinew	white feathers	
L.b. 84	wood	-	antler	sinew	no inf.	no inf.	no inf.	
L.b. 111a	wood	no inf.	no inf.	no inf.	no inf.	no inf.	no inf.	
L.b. 111b	wood	no inf.	no inf.	no inf.	no inf.	no inf.	no inf.	
L.b. 111c	wood	no inf.	no inf.	no inf.	no inf.	sinew	no inf.	
L.b. 116.1	wood	-	antler	no inf.	sinew	sinew	no inf.	
L.b. 116.2	wood	-	antler	no inf.	no inf.	sinew	dark brown	

Inv.-number	Shaft	Foreshaft	Point	Wrapping tang	Wrapping nock	Wrapping fletching	Feathers	Comment
Lb. 430a	wood	no inf.	no inf.	no inf.	no inf.	no inf.	no inf.	
Lb. 430b	wood	no inf.	no inf.	no inf.	no inf.	no inf.	no inf.	
Lb. 430c	wood	no inf.	no inf.	no inf.	no inf.	no inf.	no inf.	
Lb. 430d	wood	no inf.	no inf.	no inf.	no inf.	no inf.	no inf.	
Lb. 579	wood	-	antler	no inf.	sinew	sinew	brown feathers	
Lc. 32b	wood	-	antler	no inf.	no inf.	no inf.	no inf.	Kunstkammer
Lu. 323a	wood	-	iron	sinew	no inf.	-	-	no fletching
Lu. 323b	wood	-	iron	sinew	no inf.	-	-	no fletching
Lu. 323c	wood	-	iron	sinew	no inf.	-	-	no fletching
Lu. 323d	wood	-	iron	sinew	sinew	-	-	no fletching
Lu. 324a	wood	antler	iron	sinew	sinew	no inf.	no inf.	
Lu. 324b	wood	antler	iron	sinew	sinew	no inf.	no inf.	
Lu. 327a	wood	antler	iron	sinew	sinew	no inf.	no inf.	
Lu. 327b	wood	antler	iron	sinew	sinew	no inf.	no inf.	
Lu. 704	wood	antler	no inf.	no inf.	no inf.	no inf.	no inf.	
Lu. 705a	wood	-	antler	sinew	sinew	no inf.	no inf.	
Lu. 705b	wood	antler	iron	plant fiber	sinew	no inf.	no inf.	
x. 173c	wood	antler	iron	sinew	sinew	no inf.	no inf.	
x. 173d	wood	-	antler	sinew	sinew	no inf.	no inf.	
x. 173f	wood	antler	iron	no inf.	sinew	no inf.	no inf.	
x. 173g	wood	-	antler	plant fiber	sinew	no inf.	no inf.	
"Sukkertoppen Distr"	wood	-	antler	sinew	sinew	sinew	no inf.	
Bergen painting	wood	-	osseous	no inf.	no inf.	no inf.	no inf.	
Copenhagen painting	wood	osseous	metal	no inf.	no inf.	no inf.	no inf.	

A8 – Arrow measurements (in cm)

Measurements printed **bold** are incomplete.

Inv.-number	Total length	Length shaft	Length fore-shaft	Length Point	Length fletching	Depth string groove	Width nock	Thickness nock	Thickness shaft distal end	Thickness shaft middle	Thickness shaft proximal end	Width fore-shaft	Thickness fore-shaft	Width point	Thickness point
L 1.6657	27	no inf.	no inf.	no inf.	8	0.5	1.4	0.4	no inf.	no inf.	1.1	no inf.	no inf.	no inf.	no inf.
L 6.885	**15.1**	no inf.	no inf.	no inf.	no inf.	no inf.	no inf.	no inf.	0.9	no inf.	no inf.	no inf.	no inf.	no inf.	no inf.
L 8.1789	8	no inf.	no inf.	no inf.	no inf.	0.4	1.3	0.4	no inf.	no inf.	0.7	no inf.	no inf.	no inf.	no inf.
L 8.1839	**11.5**	no inf.	no inf.	no inf.	no inf.	0.4	**1**	**0.2**	no inf.	no inf.	0.6	no inf.	no inf.	no inf.	no inf.
L 8.1953	9.7	no inf.	no inf.	no inf.	no inf.	0.5	1.9	0.3	no inf.	no inf.	no inf.	no inf.	no inf.	no inf.	no inf.
L 8.1954	7.2	no inf.	no inf.	no inf.	no inf.	0.3	1	0.2	no inf.	no inf.	0.7	no inf.	no inf.	no inf.	no inf.
L 8.1955	9	no inf.	no inf.	no inf.	no inf.	0.3	0.7	0.2	no inf.	no inf.	0.4	no inf.	no inf.	no inf.	no inf.
L 8.1956	14.7	no inf.	no inf.	no inf.	no inf.	0.4	1.2	0.2	no inf.	no inf.	0.5	no inf.	no inf.	no inf.	no inf.
L 17.112	52.7	38.8	-	18.3	no inf.	0.4	1.5	0.3	1	1.1	0.9	1.7	0.5	1.7	0.2
L 1661	**58.6**	**58.6**	no inf.	no inf.	no inf.	0.4	1	0.5	1.1	1.0	1	no inf.	no inf.	no inf.	no inf.
L 1958.2	**60**	41.9	18.7	**3.8**	16.5	no inf.	1	0.4	1.1	1	0.9	1.1	1	1.8	0.2
L 2878a	63.4	63.4	no inf.	no inf.	20	0.3	1.6	0.9	1.4	1.4	1.4	no inf.	no inf.	no inf.	no inf.
L 2878b	57.5	57.5	no inf.	no inf.	20	0.4	1.5	0.8	1.2	1.3	1.3	no inf.	no inf.	no inf.	no inf.
L 2878c	65.2	65.2	no inf.	no inf.	22	0.4	1.4	0.7	1.2	1.2	1.2	no inf.	no inf.	no inf.	no inf.
L 2878d	64.2	64.2	no inf.	no inf.	22	0.5	1.5	0.8	1.3	1.2	1.2	no inf.	no inf.	no inf.	no inf.
L 2878e	**63.8**	63.8	no inf.	no inf.	22	0.5	1.3	0.7	1.3	1.2	1.1	no inf.	no inf.	no inf.	no inf.
L 2879a	56.3	56.3	no inf.	no inf.	no inf.	0.4	1.1	0.7	0.9	0.8	0.7	no inf.	no inf.	no inf.	no inf.
L 2879b	55.1	55.1	no inf.	no inf.	no inf.	0.4	1.2	0.6	0.9	0.8	0.8	no inf.	no inf.	no inf.	no inf.
L 2880a	**46.5**	**46.5**	no inf.	no inf.	no inf.	no inf.	no inf.	no inf.	1.3	1.2	1.1	no inf.	no inf.	no inf.	no inf.
L 2880b	**48.9**	**48.9**	no inf.	no inf.	no inf.	no inf.	no inf.	no inf.	1.2	1.1	0.9	no inf.	no inf.	no inf.	no inf.
L 2880c	**43.7**	**43.7**	no inf.	no inf.	no inf.	no inf.	no inf.	no inf.	1.3	1.3	1.2	no inf.	no inf.	no inf.	no inf.
L 2880d	**53.5**	**53.5**	no inf.	no inf.	no inf.	no inf.	no inf.	no inf.	1.2	1.1	1	no inf.	no inf.	no inf.	no inf.
L 2880e	**47.5**	**47.5**	no inf.	no inf.	no inf.	0.5	1.2	0.4	**1.1**	**1.1**	**1**	no inf.	no inf.	no inf.	no inf.
L 3663	**26.9**	no inf.	no inf.	no inf.	no inf.	0.4	2 rec.	0.3	no inf.	no inf.	0.9	no inf.	no inf.	no inf.	no inf.
Lb. 3	57.2	33	-	**24**	9	0.6	1.4	0.5	1	1.1	0.9	-	-	1.3	0.8
Lb. 84	47.7	35.7	-	13	no inf.	0.4	no inf.	0.4	1.1	0.9	0.7	-	-	1.1	0.5
Lb. 11a	**36.9**	**36.9**	no inf.	no inf.	9	0.5	1.2	0.3	1	1	0.9	no inf.	no inf.	no inf.	no inf.

Inv.-number	Total length	Length shaft	Length fore-shaft	Length Point	Length fletching	Depth string groove	Width nock	Thickness nock	Thickness shaft distal end	Thickness shaft middle	Thickness shaft proximal end	Width fore-shaft	Thickness fore-shaft	Width point	Thickness point
Lb. 111b	38	38	no inf.	no inf.	9	0.6	1.2	0.3	1	1	0.9	no inf.	no inf.	no inf.	no inf.
Lb. 111c	40.1	40.1	no inf.	no inf.	11	0.6	1.3	0.3	1.1	1	0.9	no inf.	no inf.	no inf.	no inf.
Lb. 116.1	54.8	32.7	-	24	9	0.6	1.1	0.4	1	1	0.9	-	-	1.5	0.6
Lb. 116.2	59.2	38.4	-	23	8.5	0.5	1.2	0.4	1	1.2	1	-	-	1.7	0.7
Lb. 430a	67.1	67.1	no inf.	no inf.	no inf.	0.5	1.5	0.9	1.3	1.3	1.2	no inf.	no inf.	no inf.	no inf.
Lb. 430b	59.3	59.3	no inf.	no inf.	no inf.	0.5	1.5	0.7	1.1	1	1	no inf.	no inf.	no inf.	no inf.
Lb. 430c	72.2	72.2	no inf.	no inf.	no inf.	0.5	1.4	0.7	1.2	1.2	1.2	no inf.	no inf.	no inf.	no inf.
Lb. 430d	75.9	75.9	no inf.	no inf.	20	0.5	1.4	0.7	1.3	1.2	1.2	no inf.	no inf.	no inf.	no inf.
Lb. 579	72.8	52.8	-	21	10.5	0.4	1	0.5	0.9	0.9	0.9	-	-	1.4	0.6
Lu. 323a	47.1	33.6	-	15.4	-	0.3	1.4	0.3	1.1	1	0.9	-	-	1.8	0.2
Lc. 32b	82	no inf.	-	no inf.	no inf.	no inf.	no inf.	no inf.	no inf.	no inf.	no inf.	-	-	no inf.	no inf.
Lu. 323b	47.2	32.5	-	16.8	-	0.3	1.4	0.3	1	1	0.9	-	-	1.8	0.2
Lu. 323c	53.1	37.4	-	17.7	-	0.3	1.4	0.3	1.1	1	0.9	-	-	1.8	0.2
Lu. 323d	48.6	33.8	-	17.9	-	0.3	1.3	0.3	1	1	0.9	-	-	1.6	0.2
Lu. 324a	57.8	44.9	14.6	2.9	no inf.	0.5	1.1	0.3	1.1	1	0.8	1	no inf.	18	0.1
Lu. 324b	61.2	48	15.8	3.1	no inf.	0.5	1.1	0.2	1	1.1	0.8	0.9	no inf.	1.7	0.2
Lu. 327a	48.6	35.8	13.8	5.2	no inf.	0.4	1.2	0.3	1.1	1	0.9	0.9	no inf.	2.8	0.2
Lu. 327b	47.4	36.3	12.7	3.6	no inf.	0.3	1.3	0.3	1	1.1	0.9	0.9	no inf.	2.4	0.2
Lu. 704	94	71	24	no inf.	no inf.	0.4	1.1	0.3	1	1	1	1.4	no inf.	no inf.	no inf.
Lu. 705a	49.6	38	-	15.2	no inf.	0.4	1.5	0.4	1.1	1	1	-	-	1	0.5
Lu. 705b	49.7	38.1	14.2	3.6	no inf.	0.4	1.6	0.3	1	1	1	0.9	no inf.	1.4	0.1
x. 173c	59.3	46.8	15.7	3.1	no inf.	0.5	1.4	0.4	1.2	1.1	0.9	1	no inf.	1.8	0.1
x. 173d	57.7	43.7	-	17.8	no inf.	0.3	1.3	0.3	1	1	1	-	-	1.4	0.7
x. 173f	51.8	39.5	14.8	3.7	no inf.	0.5	1.3	0.3	1.1	1	0.9	0.9	no inf.	2	0.2
x. 173g	58.3	42.6	-	19.2	no inf.	0.5	1.4	0.5	1	1.1	0.9	-	-	1.1	0.7
"Sukkertoppen Distr"	54.8	29.7	-	26	9	0.5	1.2	0.4	0.9	0.9	0.8	-	-	1.9	0.8
Bergen Painting	no inf.	no inf.	no inf.	no inf.	no inf.	no inf.	no inf.	no inf.	no inf.	no inf.	no inf.	no inf.	no inf.	no inf.	no inf.
Copenhagen Painting	no inf.	no inf.	no inf.	no inf.	no inf.	no inf.	no inf.	no inf.	no inf.	no inf.	no inf.	no inf.	no inf.	no inf.	no inf.

A9 – Arrow design

Inv.-number	Silhouette shaft	Cross section shaft	Silhouette foreshaft	Cross section foreshaft	Silhouette point	Cross section point	Silhouette nock	Cross section nock	Shape string groove	Silhouette fletching
L 1.6657	no inf.	oval	no inf.	no inf.	no inf.	no inf.	straight-sided	flattened	U	parabol
L 6.885	no inf.	oval	no inf.	no inf.	no inf.	no inf.	no inf.	no inf.	no inf.	no inf.
L 8.1789	no inf.	oval	no inf.	no inf.	no inf.	no inf.	broadened	flattened	V	no inf.
L 8.1839	no inf.	oval	no inf.	no inf.	no inf.	no inf.	broadened	flattened	U	no inf.
L 8.1953	no inf.	oval	no inf.	no inf.	no inf.	no inf.	broadened	flattened	V	no inf.
L 8.1954	no inf.	oval	no inf.	no inf.	no inf.	no inf.	broadened	flattened	V	no inf.
L 8.1955	no inf.	oval	no inf.	no inf.	no inf.	no inf.	broadened	flattened	V	no inf.
L 8.1956	no inf.	oval	no inf.	no inf.	no inf.	no inf.	broadened	flattened	V	no inf.
L 17.112	barrelled	round	-	-	lanceolate	biconvex	broadened	flattened	U	no inf.
L 1661	tapered	oval	no inf.	no inf.	no inf.	no inf.	straight-sided	flattened	U	no inf.
L 1958.2	tapered	round	tapered	oval	lanceolate	flat	straight-sided	oval	no inf.	no inf.
L 2878a	cylindrical	round	no inf.	no inf.	no inf.	no inf.	stepped	oval	U	no inf.
L 2878b	cylindrical	round	no inf.	no inf.	no inf.	no inf.	stepped	oval	U	no inf.
L 2878c	cylindrical	round	no inf.	no inf.	no inf.	no inf.	straight-sided	oval	U	no inf.
L 2878d	tapered	round	no inf.	no inf.	no inf.	no inf.	broadened	oval	V	no inf.
L 2878e	tapered	round	no inf.	no inf.	no inf.	no inf.	broadened	oval	V	no inf.
L 2879a	tapered	round	no inf.	no inf.	no inf.	no inf.	broadened	oval	U	no inf.
L 2879b	tapered	round	no inf.	no inf.	no inf.	no inf.	broadened	oval	U	no inf.
L 2880a	tapered	round	no inf.	no inf.	no inf.	no inf.	no inf.	no inf.	no inf.	no inf.
L 2880b	tapered	round	no inf.	no inf.	no inf.	no inf.	no inf.	no inf.	no inf.	no inf.
L 2880c	tapered	oval	no inf.	no inf.	no inf.	no inf.	no inf.	no inf.	no inf.	no inf.
L 2880d	tapered	round	no inf.	no inf.	no inf.	no inf.	no inf.	no inf.	no inf.	no inf.
L 2880e	tapered	oval	no inf.	no inf.	no inf.	no inf.	broadened	flattened	V	no inf.
L 3663	no inf.	oval	no inf.	no inf.	no inf.	no inf.	broadened	flattened	U	no inf.
Lb. 3	tapered	round	-	-	lanceolate	triangular	broadened	flattened	V	no inf.
Lb. 84	tapered	round	-	-	lanceolate	diamond	broadened	flattened	no inf.	no inf.
Lb. 111a	tapered	round	no inf.	no inf.	no inf.	no inf.	broadened	flattened	V	no inf.
Lb. 111b	tapered	round	no inf.	no inf.	no inf.	no inf.	broadened	flattened	V	no inf.
Lb. 111c	tapered	round	no inf.	no inf.	no inf.	no inf.	broadened	flattened	V	no inf.

Inv.-number	Silhouette shaft	Cross section shaft	Silhouette foreshaft	Cross section foreshaft	Silhouette point	Cross section point	Silhouette nock	Cross section nock	Shape string groove	Silhouette fletching
Lb. 116.1	tapered	round	-	-	lanceolate with barbs	triangular	broadened	flattened	V	no inf.
Lb. 116.2	barrelled	oval	-	-	lanceolate with barbs	triangular	broadened	flattened	V	no inf.
Lb. 430a	cylindrical	round	no inf.	no inf.	no inf.	no inf.	broadened	oval	U	no inf.
Lb. 430b	tapered	round	no inf.	no inf.	no inf.	no inf.	broadened	flattened	U	no inf.
Lb. 430c	cylindrical	round	no inf.	no inf.	no inf.	no inf.	broadened	flattened	U	no inf.
Lb. 430d	tapered	round	no inf.	no inf.	no inf.	no inf.	broadened	oval	U	no inf.
Lb. 579	cylindrical	round	-	-	lanceolate with barbs	triangular	straight-sided	flattened	V	parabol
Lu. 323a	tapered	oval	-	-	lanceolate	biconvex	broadened	flattened	V	no inf.
Lu. 323b	tapered	oval	-	-	lanceolate	biconvex	broadened	flattened	V	no inf.
Lu. 323c	tapered	round	-	-	lanceolate	biconvex	broadened	flattened	V	no inf.
Lu. 323d	tapered	oval	-	-	lanceolate	biconvex	broadened	flattened	V	no inf.
Lu. 324a	tapered	round	cylindrical	oval	triangular	flat	broadened	flattened	V	no inf.
Lu. 324b	barrelled	oval	cylindrical	round	triangular with barbs	flat	broadened	flattened	U	no inf.
Lu. 327a	tapered	oval	cylindrical	oval	lanceolate with barbs	flat	broadened	flattened	V	no inf.
Lu. 327b	barrelled	round	cylindrical	round	triangular	flat	broadened	flattened	V	no inf.
Lu. 704	cylindrical	round	broadened	drop-shaped	no inf.	no inf.	straight-sided	flattened	U	no inf.
Lu. 705a	tapered	round	-	-	lanceolate	round	broadened	flattened	U	no inf.
Lu. 705b	cylindrical	round	cylindrical	diamond-shaped	lanceolate	flat	broadened	flattened	V	no inf.
x. 173c	tapered	oval	cylindrical	round	triangular	flat	broadened	flattened	V	no inf.
x. 173d	barrelled	oval	-	-	lanceolate	diamond	broadened	flattened	U	no inf.
x. 173f	tapered	oval	cylindrical	round	lanceolate with barbs	flat	broadened	flattened	V	no inf.
x. 173g	barrelled	round	-	-	lanceolate with barbs	hexagonal	broadened	flattened	U	no inf.
"Sukkertoppen Distr"	cylindrical	round	-	-	lanceolate with barbs	biconvex	broadened	flattened	U	no inf.
Bergen painting	no inf.	no inf.	-	-	lanceolate with barbs	no inf.	no inf.	no inf.	no inf.	no inf.
Copenhagen painting	no inf.	no inf.	straight-sided with barbs	no inf.	lanceolate	no inf.	no inf.	no inf.	no inf.	trapezoidal

A10 – Arrow technology

Inv._number	Joint shaft-head	Joint foreshaft-point	Fletching method	Attachment feathers
L. 1.6657	no inf.	no inf.	tangential	wrapping
L. 6.885	closed socket, wrapping	no inf.	no inf.	no inf.
L. 8.1789	no inf.	no inf.	no inf.	no inf.
L. 8.1839	no inf.	no inf.	no inf.	no inf.
L. 8.1953	no inf.	no inf.	no inf.	no inf.
L. 8.1954	no inf.	no inf.	no inf.	no inf.
L. 8.1955	no inf.	no inf.	no inf.	no inf.
L. 8.1956	no inf.	no inf.	no inf.	no inf.
L. 17.112	split, wrapping	-	no inf.	no inf.
L. 1661	closed socket, screw, wrapping	no inf.	no inf.	no inf.
L. 1958.2	closed socket, wrapping	rivet	tangential	wrapping
L. 2878a	closed socket, wrapping	no inf.	tangential	wrapping, glue?
L. 2878b	closed socket, wrapping	no inf.	tangential	wrapping, glue?
L. 2878c	closed socket, wrapping	no inf.	tangential	wrapping, glue?
L. 2878d	closed socket, wrapping	no inf.	tangential	wrapping, glue?
L. 2878e	closed socket, wrapping	no inf.	tangential	wrapping, glue?
L. 2879a	closed socket, wrapping	no inf.	no inf.	no inf.
L. 2879b	closed socket, wrapping	no inf.	no inf.	no inf.
L. 2880a	closed socket, wrapping	no inf.	no inf.	no inf.
L. 2880b	no inf.	no inf.	no inf.	no inf.
L. 2880c	closed socket, wrapping	no inf.	no inf.	no inf.
L. 2880d	closed socket, wrapping	no inf.	no inf.	no inf.
L. 2880e	no inf.	no inf.	no inf.	no inf.
L. 3663	no inf.	no inf.	no inf.	no inf.
Lb. 3	closed socket, wrapping	-	no inf.	no inf.
Lb. 84	closed socket, screw, wrapping	-	no inf.	no inf.
Lb. 111a	closed socket, screw, wrapping	no inf.	no inf.	no inf.
Lb. 111b	closed socket, screw, wrapping	no inf.	no inf.	no inf.
Lb. 111c	closed socket, wrapping	no inf.	no inf.	no inf.
Lb. 116.1	closed socket, wrapping	-	no inf.	no inf.
Lb. 116.2	closed socket, wrapping	-	tangential	wrapping

Inv.-number	Joint shaft-head	Joint foreshaft-point	Fletching method	Attachment feathers
Lb. 430a	scarf, wrapping	no inf.	no inf.	no inf.
Lb. 430b	closed socket, screw, wrapping	no inf.	no inf.	no inf.
Lb. 430c	closed socket, screw, wrapping	no inf.	no inf.	no inf.
Lb. 430d	closed socket, screw, wrapping	no inf.	no inf.	no inf.
Lb. 579	closed socket, screw, wrapping	-	tangential	wrapping
Lc. 32b	closed socket, screw, wrapping	-	no inf.	no inf.
Lu. 323a	split, wrapping	-	-	-
Lu. 323b	split, wrapping	-	-	-
Lu. 323c	split, wrapping	-	-	-
Lu. 323d	split, wrapping	-	-	-
Lu. 324a	scarf, wrapping	rivet	no inf.	no inf.
Lu. 324b	scarf, wrapping	rivet	no inf.	no inf.
Lu. 327a	scarf, wrapping	rivet	no inf.	no inf.
Lu. 327b	scarf, wrapping	rivet	no inf.	no inf.
Lu. 704	closed socket, screw, wrapping	rivet	no inf.	no inf.
Lu. 705a	scarf, wrapping	-	no inf.	no inf.
Lu. 705b	scarf, wrapping	rivet	no inf.	no inf.
x. 173c	scarf, wrapping	rivet	no inf.	no inf.
x. 173d	scarf, wrapping	-	no inf.	no inf.
x. 173f	scarf, wrapping	rivet	no inf.	no inf.
x. 173g	scarf, wrapping	-	no inf.	no inf.
"Sukkertoppen Distr"	closed socket, screw, wrapping	-	no inf.	no inf.
Bergen painting	no inf.	-	tangential	wrapping
Copenhagen painting	no inf.	rivet	tangential	wrapping

A11 – Single antler arrowheads from West Greenland (in cm)

Measurements printed **bold** are incomplete.

Inv.-number	Source of data	Depository	Provenance	Dating	Context	Collector	Acquisition	Length	Tang form
L. 6.876	this study	National Museum of Denmark	Illutalik	16th–19th cent.	settlement	Mathiassen	1933	17.2	screw
L. 1694	this study	National Museum of Denmark	Sermermiut	no inf.	no inf.	no inf.	no inf.	18.5	screw
L. 1693	this study	National Museum of Denmark	Sermermiut	no inf.	no inf.	no inf.	no inf.	19.0	screw
L. 1695a	this study	National Museum of Denmark	Sermermiut	no inf.	no inf.	no inf.	no inf.	20.0	screw
L. 1695b	this study	National Museum of Denmark	Sermermiut	no inf.	no inf.	no inf.	no inf.	18.5	screw
L. 1696	this study	National Museum of Denmark	Sermermiut	no inf.	no inf.	no inf.	no inf.	26.5	screw
L. 2818	this study	National Museum of Denmark	Northeast Disko	no inf.	no inf.	Zool. Museum Copenhagen	1906	32.5	2 staggered knobs
L. 2819	this study	National Museum of Denmark	Northeast Disko	no inf.	no inf.	Zool. Museum Copenhagen	1906	21.6	2 staggered knobs
L. 2820	this study	National Museum of Denmark	Northeast Disko	no inf.	no inf.	Zool. Museum Copenhagen	1906	24.4	2 staggered knobs
L. 2821	this study	National Museum of Denmark	Northeast Disko	no inf.	no inf.	Zool. Museum Copenhagen	1906	**22.7**	2 staggered knobs
L. 2822	this study	National Museum of Denmark	Northeast Disko	no inf.	no inf.	Zool. Museum Copenhagen	1906	24.5	2 staggered knobs
L. 2823	this study	National Museum of Denmark	Northeast Disko	no inf.	no inf.	Zool. Museum Copenhagen	1906	17.8	2 staggered knobs
L. 2824	this study	National Museum of Denmark	Northeast Disko	no inf.	no inf.	Zool. Museum Copenhagen	1906	22.5	2 staggered knobs
L. 2825	this study	National Museum of Denmark	Northeast Disko	no inf.	no inf.	Zool. Museum Copenhagen	1906	25.5	2 staggered knobs
L. 2826	this study	National Museum of Denmark	Northeast Disko	no inf.	no inf.	Zool. Museum Copenhagen	1906	19.3	2 staggered knobs
L. 2827	this study	National Museum of Denmark	Northeast Disko	no inf.	no inf.	Zool. Museum Copenhagen	1906	21.7	2 staggered knobs

Inv.-number	Source of data	Depository	Provenance	Dating	Context	Collector	Acquisition	Length	Tang form
L. 2828	this study	National Museum of Denmark	Northeast Disko	no inf.	no inf.	Zool. Museum Copenhagen	1906	24.7	2 staggered knobs
L. 2829	this study	National Museum of Denmark	Northeast Disko	no inf.	no inf.	Zool. Museum Copenhagen	1906	14.4	2 staggered knobs
L. 2831	this study	National Museum of Denmark	Northeast Disko	no inf.	no inf.	Zool. Museum Copenhagen	1906	22.0	2 staggered knobs
L. 2832	this study	National Museum of Denmark	Northeast Disko	no inf.	no inf.	Zool. Museum Copenhagen	1906	20.6	2 staggered knobs
L. 2833	this study	National Museum of Denmark	Northeast Disko	no inf.	no inf.	Zool. Museum Copenhagen	1906	23.9	2 staggered knobs
L. 2834	this study	National Museum of Denmark	Northeast Disko	no inf.	no inf.	Zool. Museum Copenhagen	1906	27.7	2 staggered knobs
L. 2860	this study	National Museum of Denmark	West Greenland	no inf.	no inf.	no inf.	no inf.	23.7	screw
L. 2869	this study	National Museum of Denmark	West Greenland	no inf.	no inf.	no inf.	no inf.	22.0	screw
L. 2874	this study	National Museum of Denmark	West Greenland	no inf.	no inf.	no inf.	no inf.	18.7	screw
L. 2875	this study	National Museum of Denmark	West Greenland	no inf.	no inf.	no inf.	no inf.	25.0	screw
L. 2876	this study	National Museum of Denmark	West Greenland	no inf.	no inf.	no inf.	no inf.	20.5	screw
L. 2877	this study	National Museum of Denmark	West Greenland	no inf.	no inf.	no inf.	no inf.	27.9	screw
L. 9140	this study	National Museum of Denmark	Uummannaq	no inf.	grave	no inf.	no inf.	22.2	screw
L. 9141	this study	National Museum of Denmark	Uummannaq	no inf.	grave	no inf.	no inf.	23.7	screw
L. 9148	this study	National Museum of Denmark	Uummannaq	no inf.	grave	no inf.	no inf.	29.1	screw
Lb. 54a	this study	National Museum of Denmark	West Greenland	no inf.	no inf.	Zimmer	1856	29.1	screw
Lb. 54b	this study	National Museum of Denmark	West Greenland	no inf.	no inf.	Zimmer	1856	**29.4**	screw
Lb. 55	this study	National Museum of Denmark	West Greenland	no inf.	no inf.	Zimmer	1856	29.9	screw
Lb. 79	this study	National Museum of Denmark	West Greenland	no inf.	grave	Pfaff	1863	24.0	screw